COMMON SENSE ABOUT
CHRISTIAN ETHICS

COMMON SENSE ABOUT CHRISTIAN ETHICS

by

EDWARD CARPENTER

LONDON
VICTOR GOLLANCZ LTD
1961

To David, Michael, Paul
—and Louise: in spite of
whose constant interruptions
this book has been written

Printed in Great Britain by
The Camelot Press Ltd., London and Southampton

CONTENTS

PREFACE

THE FOLLOWING IS not a text book on ethics. If it were so, a great deal of philosophical discussion which has deliberately been omitted would need to be included. Rather it is an effort to see the problem of a specifically Christian ethic within the context of a full Christian Faith. It is for this reason, and because of the particular attitude that I have taken throughout, that an excursion into history has been necessary.

The reader who expects to find a cut and dried answer to every contemporary moral problem will, I fear, be bitterly disappointed, for it is one of the basic contentions of this book that Christian Faith cannot supply it, and that it would not be a good thing for us if it could. On the other hand, it is equally a contention of this book that Christianity stands for a personal order in an ordered Kingdom.

In a short work of this kind a lapse into generalities, and sometimes into a seeming dogmatism, has not been entirely avoided. For this I must apologise. The alternative would have been considerably to limit my field and this I did not wish to do.

One subject has not been dealt with at all, namely, the confrontation of the ethical patterns in Christianity and Buddhism, now that they are living together side by side in various parts of the world. No subject could be more important, but to do it justice would have meant the writing of another book.

EDWARD CARPENTER

March 1961

I: MAINLY BACKGROUND

CHAPTER I

IS THERE A CHRISTIAN ETHIC?

IF COMMON SENSE IS not easily come by, yet most of us have a shrewd idea what it is, and can recognise a person who has it: but to talk of Christian ethics raises a problem concerning which different people will have a variety of things to say. Taken at its face value, the juxtaposition of these two words suggests that there is a particular pattern of behaviour, or motivation to right conduct, which is peculiarly Christian, in the sense that it arises out of, or is organically related to, Christian Faith.

But is this true? And if it is, in what way is it true? It might be argued that the example of Jesus is binding on his followers, and that Jesus lived out, and laid down, a unique ethic. Or it might be said that fundamental Christian doctrine presupposes certain truths about the nature of man—what he is like—and henceforth how he ought to behave. Or again it might be maintained that Christianity furnishes no new ethic, but more powerful incentives to persuade men to live up to a commonly accepted moral code.

But whatever precise form this claim to uniqueness may take, basically it must maintain that there is something distinctive in Christian ethics over against other ethical systems. Yet I ask again, is this true? And if it is true, should we be equally justified in talking of Buddhist ethics, Mohammedan ethics, Communist ethics—and so on, the inference being that different religious faiths, or ideological systems, generate their own patterns of behaviour and consequent moral criteria. Some doubtless who say "yes" to this question would, however, wish to qualify their assent by adding that though various faiths, particularly the great world religions, may differ in the minutiae of their ethical systems, yet in the great fundamentals they are agreed. All of them exalt the truth over the lie; justice over injustice. All encourage responsible and (as they see it) noble living.

Many are the sincerely religious people who hold this latter view and have held it across the centuries. For example, eighteenth-century thinkers, under the influence of contemporary deism, maintained (as did Thomas Aquinas centuries before) that there is a natural religion, and that the unassisted reason is capable of proving the existence of God, and establishing a universally valid pattern of right conduct.

Some of these deists went on to say that the Christian Faith uniquely gave power to live out this code, but they admitted that it did not invent the code itself. Bishop Charles Gore, from a very different point of view, argued in his *The Philosophy of the Good Life* (1930), that the basic agreement of the great religions as to what constitutes the good life was itself impressive testimony both to its reality and objectivity.

For different reasons, though in similar vein, the tendency of a great deal of contemporary thought has been to play down the suggestion that the uniqueness of the Christian Faith is to be found in its particular moral insights. It will be necessary to discuss this later: and to ask how true is the oft repeated assertion that there is nothing unique in Jesus as an ethical teacher; that nearly all he proclaimed in this field can be found in the Old Testment, in the Upanishads of India, or indeed in Plato; and that what is really significant in Jesus is not the ethics which he may have proclaimed, but the divine status from which he proclaimed them.

Thus the contemporary mood is still one of strong reaction against the "liberal Christ" of the nineteenth century, and the resulting tendency is therefore to find the uniqueness of Jesus elsewhere than in his moral leadership. Indeed, many scholars deplore the giving of any emphasis to this aspect of his ministry.

The effect of this latter attitude upon the rank and file of Christians is, almost inevitably, to dissuade them from looking for distinctive Christian moral insights or expecting their Faith to say anything significant when it comes to making judgements on contemporary issues.

A great deal of this book (either directly or indirectly) will therefore be concerned with a group of related questions which may be most simply put as follows: "Is there a specifically Christian ethic?" If there is not, ought we more properly to think in terms of behaviour-patterns to which all men of good-will, irrespective of whether they make any religious profession, are prepared to give their assent. If the latter, where does the Christian Faith come in?

Such questions are, perhaps, not quite so straightforward as they at first seem: though it is still necessary to ask them. Certainly if there is a particular Christian ethic we should expect it to require a man to adopt a distinctive attitude to his fellows; that is, to experience a compulsion which would not necessarily constrain him unless he had made a prior commitment to the "way of Jesus". Further, if there is such a Christian ethic, its sanction will not be found in commonly accepted general principles, but in particular Christian truths. Indeed it might be, though this would not necessarily follow, that some of its ethical imperatives would appear "foolishness" to those who do not accept the Christian Faith as authoritative.

If on the other hand, it is true that there are no moral norms[1] which are unique to Christianity, then the Christian must be content if his Faith gives him greater power to live up to whatever standard is generally accepted as the highest; and if, at the

[1] By norm I mean, roughly, a rule or recognised standard.

same time, it provides him with more stimulating incentives to embark upon this high endeavour. Perhaps I might, at this point, illustrate both points of view, maybe in a slightly concentrated form.

An example of the first is the familiar claim that no valid case can be made for pacifism unless it is based upon a specifically Christian theology of the Cross.

An example of the second may be taken from a much discussed contemporary issue—that of capital punishment. Without falling back upon any definite Christian insight, many have asserted that capital punishment is intrinsically immoral, disgustingly squalid, and monumentally stupid—immoral in that it inflicts intolerable mental agony without an absolute proved necessity; squalid in that the whole apparatus of the death cell and the hangman is offensive; stupid in that there is something preposterous in assuming that society can get out of any real social problem by killing one of its members.

Some Christians, however, who accept the above arguments would yet go further and maintain, from the premises of Christian Faith, that capital punishment is an impiety, since it is an extreme example of creaturely and sinful man arrogating to himself the final sovereignty of God.

In the above two illustrations, we have one ethical attitude which can only be asserted (so it is claimed) from within a full Christian Faith: and another to which Christian Faith gives an added support.

The problem as to whether there is, or is not, any particular Christian ethic thus raises a question so fundamental that it will need frank and careful discussion. So far as the man in the street is concerned, I think there is little doubt that whenever he turns his mind to ethical problems he has an instinctive feeling that there *ought* to be a distinctively Christian attitude, though this is not to say that he would welcome it if there were!

As it is, he experiences a certain bemusement when he sees the Christian Churches apparently unable to contribute much that is distinctive concerning so many things that are in debate in the modern world. When it comes to the manufacture of hydrogen bombs, such guidance as is given is usually couched in general and ambiguous terms and offers little practical help. It is dangerous to try to meet every popular demand since the cry for authoritative guidance is not usually healthy or adult: but at least to nourish the hope that something a little more definite might come from the Christian Church is understandable if optimistic. Ordinary people do ask of their Faith that it should help them in the situation in which they are, and at the point of their own need. In the contemporary world great problems, arising out of the collective life, are of concern to everyone, since everyone is necessarily involved in them. Though the man in the street may not use the same language, he might well ask with Dr. Nils Ehrenström: "Is a distinctively Christian judgement on the structure of society possible, or does this apply only to the motives of persons acting within this structure? . . . May there be a difference in the will of God for a Christian concerning his action as a private person and his action in his official capacity? Can the Christian commandment of love be realised in all spheres of life? If not, what are the limits of such realisation and what alternative principles are applicable and binding (e.g. justice and loyalty)?".

This reference to the collective life may serve as the jumping-off ground for our enquiry. When Plato, in perhaps his most famous work *The Republic*, sets out to ask what "justice" is, he makes Socrates suggest that the quest may be best pursued by asking what is meant by a "just state". Justice becomes clearer (since justice anyhow is a social concept) when it is magnified, and seen in a broader context, at more than life size. The same approach may be valuable in respect of Christian ethics, since religion also relates to the social life, and Christianity, in particular, has the distinction of helping to generate the particular political and cultural pattern of Western Europe. Whatever is distinctive in Christianity may be the more easily seen when its results are writ large in a civilisation: and when this civilisation is compared with others. Of course, such a brief enquiry presents difficulties because it is easy to lapse into facile generalities, and always hard to isolate causative factors. It is certainly worth making, however, so long as the tentative nature of the conclusions is recognised. Judgements of this kind are always precarious but it is essential to make them.

CHAPTER II

EAST AND WEST

A FAITH OR IDEOLOGY, no matter what its character, cannot be confined in its influence to the person who commits himself to it. We may take it that the social urge is inherent in man and that the collective life of society arises naturally out of the physical as well as the instinctive and psychical needs of humanity. For this reason a faith which commands the allegiance of the hearts and minds of men, be it a collective horror (like Nazism) or a private pietism (like some mysticisms) will have its inevitable repercussions upon society as a whole. Nor does it matter, in this respect, whether the faith leads to conscious manipulation and direction of society (as in Christianity), or whether it encourages withdrawal from society (as in Buddhism): still its influence will be formative. It is quite impossible to isolate or screen off individuals from the community in which they live.

Nor is there any need to try to separate the pressure of the environment *upon* man, from the effect upon that environment of a "dawning desire" *in* man. They are both obviously formative, and it is impossible to say where one begins and the other ends. Ideologies, if they are in part evoked by the total environment, yet proceed to affect, and subtly to change, that environment: and the fact that the ideology may claim to be world-renouncing does not mean, for a moment, that it ceases to influence the world from which it encourages its initiates to escape. Its influence will be negatively formative but none the less real and effective.

The character of a civilisation, therefore, will provide some clue as to the long term effects, and consequently the nature, of the dominant ideology (ethical pattern) which has been at work within it.

It is customary, when taking stock of world civilisation, to make a broad contrast between East and West—between Europe on the one hand, and China and India on the other. This is a useful popular distinction so long as it is not pushed too far— that is so long as it is remembered that what they have in common is as important as that which divides them. All great civilisations stand for some ordered pattern of collective living: for some kind of stability: for the possibility of consciously directing society towards the good life, no matter how that good life is conceived. In this latter respect they enshrine a concept of value, expressed either in law or custom: and they represent an assertion of the corporate life which is not confined to instinctive biological urges. They treat men as in some sense transcending their natural environment. "Society comes into existence that man may live. It continues in order that he may live well."

Yet though civilisations have a great deal in common, it is equally true that they differ, not only in those things which may reasonably be regarded as trivial and unimportant but also in the more significant aspects of their total life.

Thus it is significant that, in general, Eastern civilisations have become static when they once arrived, whereas Western civilisation has proved itself to be dynamic—that is in a state of constant movement, even when governmental direction has striven to preserve an equilibrium. The Eastern temperament, or psychology, has shown itself, in the main, to be withdrawing, contemplative, and at times mystical: whereas Western psychology, in its general expression, has been activist and practical. If men in the East have been prone to turn inwards in order to explore the depths and richness of their own being (to find the Absolute, the Unchanging), Western man has looked outwards to the world and his brother man. One explores the universe within; the other the universe without.

Of course, such broad contrast cannot be true in quite this stark sense. It is all a matter of degree, of subtle shades of emphasis. Yet the fact remains that over vast areas in the East civilisations have tended to remain without change for centuries, and that this equilibrium has continued in spite of apparently intolerable suffering and terrible squalor. What arose out of the economic needs of one age has persisted into another when the necessity had passed and the system had become an oppressive anachronism. It seems impossible not to connect this historical inertia, at least in part, with a habit of mind, the cultivation of a spirit of detachment to which external change is abhorrent. The caste system, for example, once undoubtedly discharged a useful social and economic function: it has lingered on, and proved obstinately resistant to reform, because the temperament bred in the East provided, if not a rationale, at least a disinclination to do anything practical about it. Why worry? The wise man is indifferent to external fortune, and maybe in the rhythmic and ceaseless flow of Karma retribution is worked out this way. The present can be explained as a result of the inevitable necessities of the past.

When we turn to the West, in which three influences have been largely formative—the Greek philosophic tradition, Roman law and government, and the Hebraic-Christian emphasis on the living God—we notice certain distinctive features.

First, Christian Western civilisation has been in a constant state of movement. The equilibrium of one age has seldom survived to give form to the next. To use Hegel's dialectic, synthesis, once established, has soon broken up again into thesis and antithesis. Even during the Middle Ages, when official Christian teaching saw life essentially as a pilgrimage to a better land, and when theological sanctions tried to preserve a status quo, such conservatism was finally ineffective to prevent change. The Kingdom of God could not be entirely relegated to the next world, for it is within this present order that the traveller is shaped and fitted for the celestial city. He must therefore use time, and make the most of the opportunities with which it provides him—and this means a readiness to accept the new and the novel.

Secondly, Christian Europe has given birth to that investigation of the physical universe which is generally understood as modern science. In the popular regard this is its most spectacular and distinctive achievement. No other civilisation has done this, nor shown either the curiosity or the confidence to employ the inductive method which has brought it about. Behind this scientific achievement stands a particular temper of mind, a mental attitude which prompts and sustains it. Nothing happened in the external world sufficient to effect this psychological change, but something happened in men. The Greeks nearly got there—but not quite—and they must not be given the credit because of their comeback at the Renaissance.

Along with this intellectual curiosity, this desire to investigate the physical universe, has gone the concern to use the results to confer increasing material (and spiritual) benefits upon mankind. Pure and applied science have walked together hand in hand and together have produced our modern technological society.

Thirdly, Christian Europe has given birth to the idea of democracy as a regulative political and social ideal. Never before in history has an effort been made, on such a grand scale, to confer political status, cultural opportunity and material welfare upon the common man. No mature person needs to be reminded of the difficulties attendant upon such an attempt—the temptation to lower standards, the pressure to conformity, and so on. Yet behind the democratic ideal (which is far more than a political slogan) there is the deep conviction that every man has worth and significance: that he ought not to be treated merely as a means to an end: that he is a bearer of value. It was this conviction which finally abolished slavery—though it took a long time. As part of this awareness of individual people, and their unique needs, has gone an emphasis on compassion which has led to the growth of the hospital, and the progressive riddance of torture from penal systems. No previous age, it may be, has generated so much sheer kindliness as is common today.

Here, then, are three ingredients (possibly there are others) which may be taken as characteristic of European civilisation— that is a committal to the time-world and to history: an investigation of the physical universe by inductive methods and the using of the results for the supposed benefit of man: and the creation of the democratic ideal which gives every man value, rights, and responsibility.

It will be necessary, in a moment, to ask how far these distinctive ingredients have their counterparts in particular Christian affirmations, and what that relationship means in the sphere of ethical behaviour. But first it is necessary to strike a cautionary note, for it would be too much to claim that these different emphases between East and West have arisen solely out of distinctive faiths or philosophies. Other influences have obviously proved formative—climatic, racial and so on. Nor must Toynbee's basic thesis be forgotten—that it is stimulus and the right degree of challenge which beget change; and that where there is no challenge (for example when a community is geographically isolated) or when the challenge is too severe (as in the frozen north) civilisations do not tend to develop. Yet this does not rule out the vital contribution made by men's deepest convictions in shaping the social and cultural pattern in which they live. A teleology may draw men as well as an environment condition them. What is certainly true is that the differences which mark off East from West are reflected in the distinctive faiths which have lived in these civilisations— Hinduism, Confucianism and Buddhism in the one, Christianity (with its historic antecedents) in the other. Such general terms as world renouncing and world conquering (though these terms ought to be used with some caution and with a right understanding of what they imply) do represent real psychological and spiritual differences of approach between these two sets of faiths.

As a commentary on this assertion, it is significant that it was not until the West, particularly in the form of Communism (Christianity in a distorted form since it has the same emphasis on historic development), invaded the East, that the teeming millions of those huge regions began to ask for a higher material standard of living and for greater opportunities than their traditional and static pattern of collective life had made possible.

Perhaps it is tragic, as Toynbee suggests, that the Christian West should have finally captivated the East in the debased (or one-sided) sociology of Western technology, divorced from the fullness of the Faith; but no one can deny that it has happened. Eastern religions, by very reason of their preoccupation with the unchanging world of absolute reality, have taken the drive and the momentum out of social and national life. They have diverted and withdrawn energies elsewhere. By insisting upon Nirvana, the losing of personal identity, as the "end", they have allowed Karma to work itself out into what, for practical purposes, may be regarded as personal extinction. Karma has converted time almost into a dead-end, and has left no creative and worth-while community-goal for history to realise. True, if, as a result of such withdrawal, the East has lived with degrading poverty and intolerable social conditions, the West, in professing an activist faith, has proved predatory and aggressive. Indulging in the most vicious and sometimes fratricidal of wars, Christian Europe has for centuries been an unholy cockpit.

Yet in respect of both East and West, it is a case of the corruption of the highest. Caste and social squalor have been to the one what war, conquest and materialism have been to the other. In cultivating serenity and detachment, with the ethical attitude that goes along with them, the East has too often generated a practical indifference and apathy. The West, by encouraging committal to history, finds itself unleashing energies and prompting ambitions that it is not always able to control. Inspiring men to express their particularity, it all too easily breeds violence. The truth is that it is easier to prompt men to be activist than it is to use that activity for worthwhile ends. Christianity demands both and they must go together.

If (as I believe) the possibilities of Western living are more splendid, its corruptions are correspondingly more dangerous. If it offers greater scope to build a Kingdom it the more easily invites catastrophe: by insisting that history can be made to serve a purpose, it tempts to ambition; in so far as it encourages investigation of the physical universe, it may easily be mistaken for saying that a man's life consists in the abundance of things which he possesses.

So have Buddhism and Confucianism played their part in conditioning the East, as Christianity has done the West. It is necessary now to look at this latter Faith and to see what there is within it which has helped to generate a distinctive European civilisation. If there is a Christian ethic, it will arise organically out of distinctive Christian truth, and it is against these broader sweeps of the Christian perspective that it must be seen.

II: MAINLY BIBLICAL

CHAPTER III

THE BIBLICAL VIEW OF MAN

EVERY ETHICAL SYSTEM presupposes, indeed is organically related to, some conception of man's nature and final destiny. This conception realises itself in, and helps to mould, the collective pattern in which it is incarnated, so that society as a whole is a reflection on the grand scale of the values which men within it set out to realise—a baffling and often distorted reflection, maybe, but none the less a reflection. We have glanced at this reflection in the civilisation of the West and asked ourselves what was distinctive about it. We now turn to that dynamic ingredient working within it which has contributed largely to that distinction. This may be best undertaken by referring to the book which all Christians recognise as largely formative of their general tradition—that is, the Bible. It will be the endeavour of this chapter to find out from it what picture of man it sets before us, bearing in mind what has been suggested earlier as to the activism and historic commitment in the West.

The first thing that impresses even the most casual reader when he turns from studying the Upanishads to the Bible is the striking contrast between them in their general atmosphere and tone. The former are subtly intellectual and cosmic in their scope. The following short extract, taken almost at random, illustrates this point:

"Only those of tranquil mind, and none else, can attain abiding joy, by realising within their souls the Being who manifests one essence in a multiplicity of forms."

In contrast, the Bible moves in a world caught up in what has been aptly described as "the scandal of particularity". In this respect, the Bible is not a subtle book; it is certainly not an intellectual's book. It is not concerned with "universals", with general principles of moral behaviour, with different grades of being, with astral bodies—and so on. It deals with the concrete; the particular; the historical; the personal; as may be seen in the following verses taken from the Book of Genesis:

"Now the Lord had said unto Abraham, Get thee out of thy country, and from thy kindred, and from thy father's house: Into a land that I will show thee: And I will make of thee a great nation. . . . So Abraham departed, as the Lord had spoken unto him: And Lot went with him: And Abraham was seventy and five years old when he departed out of Haran!"[1]

Throughout the Bible, from beginning to end, runs a concrete thread of particular history. A drama is unfolded, and on to the stage there step men, some good, some bad: and as a backcloth to their appearance, though it is in fact part of the "act", is the strife of nations, some of whom are seeking world empire, others struggling, and not always successfully, to preserve a precarious independence.

The Upanishads are not geared to history in this direct way. The truths to which they bear witness are independent of this changing human scene. Indeed, it is, in the main, by retreating from history into the deeps of the self that man is perfected and redeemed. The Bible is quite otherwise: and it is this contrast which often makes it, not so much a difficult book (for it is easy to read) but a challenging one. Given, concrete, human experience has always the untidiness, the rough edges, often the misshapeness of particular things: and in the Bible this particularity is seen to assert itself within, and sometimes in defiance of, the sovereign purposes of God. As Frederick Dennison Maurice wrote of the Scriptures: "Nothing is taught by decree; everything by life and experiment".

This is another way of saying that the Bible is not a treatise

[1] Gen. xii, 1-4.

or a text book. The truth that it conveys is never found in a pure or unmixed form. All is particular, the particularity of moments in space and time; of particular people; of a particular nation; of a particular cross. When God Himself, in the fullness of time, enters uniquely into this changing human scene, it is not through the bestowal of some general enlightenment, but through incarnation in a particular person. Jesus is no universal, cosmic man, in whom individuality has been shuffled off, though some "spiritists" would have us believe so. He is, in the Gospel portrait (and we have no other), sharply defined, rich in his uniqueness. His utterances have a crisp and decisive ring about them.

It is from this jumping-off ground that we now turn to the first and basic implication of scriptural testimony—namely, its insistence on the reality of people in their particularity. On this fundamental assertion a Christian ethic, if it exists, must be built, and it will be necessary, therefore, to examine this affirmation in some detail. To make the Christian view stand in bolder relief, it may help if we contrast it with Plato's picture of the nature of a person.

To Plato there are three ultimate realities: (1) the eternal forms, of which beauty, truth, goodness, and love are pre-eminent: (2) undifferentiated matter, pure formlessness or chaos: (3) that principle of energy, creative force, call it what you will, by which form and matter are brought into relationship. There is no metaphysical or organic relationship between the three. The forms are static: they do not direct the process of change to which matter is subjected.

Such a philosophy, of necessity, conditions Plato's view about people. He sees them as pure form "imprisoned in a house of clay". The wise man, therefore, will emancipate himself from the changes and chances of this fleeting world simply in order that he may see "Reality" as it is. Against the background of such a cosmic view, it will be readily understood that a person has no final value in terms of his separateness and uniqueness. The body is a prison and, for man, fulfilment only comes through escape from it. What finally constitutes the splendour of man (his value) is just that spark of the divine essence (the forms) which is incarnated in his earthly tabernacle: but this spark is universal, undifferentiated: it is not particular: it varies only quantitively. John Smith is not so very different from Jack Jones.

Such a view, ennobling as it may seem, does not, however, finally encourage a man to redeem time, that is creatively to use it. Rather he is persuaded to contract out of its entanglement in order to contemplate a timeless perfection. It is not surprising that Plato has no philosophy of history. In so far as history moves, its rhythm is cyclic.

The Eastern attitude is even more extreme. Common to the myriad ways in which it is expressed, there is the profound conviction that deep down within every man is the cosmic self, the universal soul: and that this can be entered into through the right introspective techniques, leading to detachment from the more limited self. As raindrops lose their separate identity when they fall into the mighty ocean, so does the soul (self) finally fall back into the universal, undifferentiated whole. The initiate seeking fulfilment cultivates that expertise by and through which alone his particular self withers and dies away as an isolated centre of self-consciousness. To be re-absorbed into the vast whole, to cease to exist as a separate and therefore (almost by definition) an unfulfilled person—this is the End, Nirvana, in which desire, and all the suffering which goes along with it, cease and "the weary are at rest". This attitude must condition relations with people. What is particular in them is unimportant.

According to this view the category of personality (the cause of all the trouble!) is a limiting one. In its finiteness it bears painful witness to the ephemeral and the passing. Only by transcending it can release come. To be aware of oneself as a person is to be cut off from the great source of all life and as such to experience introversion, with all the frustrations that accompany it. It is as if a leaf were to think of itself as existing in its own right and were to act accordingly, forgetful that it is but one manifestation of the total life of the tree. The particularity of the leaf is but for a moment. When, as needs must happen, it falls and decays, it returns to the element from whence it came. So for man, his personality must be merged in a greater whole in order that a more pervasive cosmic life may assert its fuller being.

Such pantheism undoubtedly makes an appeal to sensitive people who are conscious at times of isolation, and yet have a strong urge to community.

In essence, however, it is not the Christian view, nor can a really informed (or legitimate) Christian ethic be built upon such an anthropology. The Christian approach can, perhaps, be best seen if we turn to the Biblical myth of Creation as it is given in the Book of Genesis. Here the story begins with no threefold pluralism as in Plato, but with the One God, the substantial ground of all that is. When He creates, there is no reality other than Himself, no self-existing undifferentiated matter, alien and resistant to the equally primordial forms, which he must take into account. He is limited only by the necessities of His own being—to use a Kantian phrase—or by such limitation as He imposes upon Himself.

"In the beginning God created the heaven and the earth,"— such are the grand opening words of the Creation myth in the Old Testament. No affirmation could be more significant for a Christian ethic.

The doctrine of Divine creation *ex nihilo*, and by an act of will, implies that creation does not result from a necessary overflow of, or degeneration from, the Divine Being. God is metaphysically distinct from His universe and He sees that what He creates is "very good". This means that in a truly Christian ethic there can be no suggestion that the flesh as such, that is the physical and instinctive life, is evil: or that the Christian must retreat from living. Asceticism, as an end in itself, ethical puritanism, withdrawal because the world is necessarily evil—these are incompatible with a Divine creation, *ex nihilo*. Distinctions of good and evil (value judgements) become legitimate in a way that they can never be in any pantheistic system, or when creation is seen as a necessary completion of the Divine Being. That God, who is the God of order, has by an act of will created an independent world of nature serves to encourage rational man to investigate it. The universe can be rationally explored, and with confidence.

Into this essential framework, we can now fit the Biblical picture of man's nature. In the Genesis myth, we see God taking dust of the ground, breathing into it the breath of his own life, and man thereby becoming a living soul. "And God said, Let us make man in our image, after our likeness: So God created man in his own image, in the image of God created he him; male and female created he them."

No pre-existent soul waits to be imprisoned in a house of clay. From the decisive, willed activity of God, a new creature results —man, a person, and the richness of his being results from the goodness of the Divine Will.

The Bible knows little of a metaphysical dualism of body and soul. Indeed, in Old Testament psychology the distinction between the two is not in fact made, since psychical activity and emotional feeling can be located in almost any organ or function of the body. Even the liver may wax sentimental It is the totality of man as a living sentient being, using the world which God has made, in conformity with, or in rebellion against, His

will, which constitutes the necessary pre-supposition of the
divine-human drama which the Scriptures unfold. Adam and
Eve have their place within nature, being caught up in the flux
and change of this passing world. Yet at the same time they
transcend nature in the freedom of the image of God which is
their glory. It is the tension that this ambiguity engenders (it is
something quite other than a crude opposition of flesh to spirit,
since it implies no metaphysical dualism) which creates the
conditions of the moral struggle in which men necessarily
engage.

Yet the limitation inherent in creatureliness (i.e. man is not
God) is nowhere conceived of as bound up with man's particularity, that is with his being a person. Indeed, God Himself
(Ultimate Reality) is depicted, not as the inclusive Absolute, but
as person. Though He is the supreme mystery: though His
thoughts are not our thoughts nor His ways our ways: yet in
the fullness of His own Being, He includes, raised doubtless to
the "nth" dimension, that which we should understand as the
personal in us.

The conclusion to be drawn from this is obvious. The higher
we ascend in the scale of being, the more intensely personal
being becomes, and at the same time the more sharply defined.
It is the lower forms of life which hardly differentiate themselves
from the environment around them, and do not lift themselves
up into distinctive conscious being.

So central is this truth, that a full Christian theology is
prepared to go even further and to assert that within the Being
of God Himself there are real and effective distinctions which
we can best (though still inadequately) conceive of as the distinctions which obtain between persons. The love of the Father
eternally begets the Son, which energising love returns, through
the Spirit, back to its source or ground in the Father. There is,
as the Athanasian creed says, no confusion of persons: no

B

aggression of one against the other. In God, the problem of the one and the many is resolved, not by the obliteration of distinctions, but by their confronting one another in that mutual respect for the integrity of the other which is essential to the perfect realisation of love.

The doctrine of the Trinity gives to personality an absolute value, making it a final category, part of the great and basic structure of spiritual reality itself. At no higher level is it transcended. Indeed, precisely the opposite is the case. Perfect personality exists *only* in God.

To be a person is to be "particular", and the Bible is full of this emphasis from beginning to end. It reaches a grand climax in the teaching of Jesus. The very hairs of our head are all numbered. The sheep which are mass to the human eye are individual to God—and they are known by name. God is so prodigal in creation that He never reproduces like to like. God creates separate and highly individualised existences, uniquely personal, and capable of relationships with each other and with Him. The image of God is not a mere common ingredient: it is something to be realised, in each case, as a unique element in an embracing unity.

Emphasis on "particularity" and the unique worth of a person, must not be confused, however, with any form of atavistic individualism. The personal life, so the trinitarian conception itself illustrates, is essentially social in character: it means relationship. Christianity recognises that man is by nature a social animal; and that it is within the matrix or womb of society that the rich individuality of man is given opportunity to develop and to become itself. Indeed, in the Old Testament the recognition of particularity in people comes relatively late in the story of Jewish national development. God first deals with His people as a whole. The individual has status and significance only because he belongs to the community. It is only later, with the advent of the great prophets, that the individual person is thought of as entering into a personal relation with God, and so becomes significant. Thus Jeremiah proclaimed: "In those days they shall say no more, the fathers have eaten a sour grape and the children's teeth are set on edge, but everyone shall die for his own iniquity."[1]

This leap forward into responsible personalism must therefore be seen within the context of an equal emphasis on the significance of the community. The individual must never be thought of as isolated: and when the prophet despairs of the nation as a whole, he turns in hope to a "righteous remnant", thus calling a new community into existence to replace the old. The nation, in its internal relations, is of concern to God: and its members, uniquely valuable, uniquely contribute to the fullness of its corporate life. The prophets do not disdain to talk of social justice.

Along with this Biblical teaching on the significance of man as a person and in the full splendour of his particularity, there also goes the insistence (perhaps it is more accurate to say the basic assumption) that man is a centre of free spontaneous energy, capable of directing his own life from within. The Bible just does not make sense unless this fact is taken for granted.

How man in this final sense *can* be free is indeed a mystery. No philosophy which pretends to be logically coherent can hope to find room for it; since there can be no demonstrable proof that the will is capable of making free and undetermined choices. The fact, of course, is that freedom cannot be contained with any purely rational system. If it exists, it just *is*. All we can say, if pressed, is that we *know* that we are free in the same way that we know we exist: the sense of it is given in immediate experience and is involved in self-consciousness.

But to be free does not of course mean to be absolutely free.

[1] Jer. xxxi, 29.

It is enough that a man can assert a freedom to shape the general pattern of his life in response to the choices that he makes. The area in which such choices can be effective may well be small; but in making them a man is not entirely determined by his life history to date. We are not "as old as our arteries and as good as our glands".

This fact of man's final freedom, which is basic to the Christian ethical view, raises, of course, many problems concerning which there is no formal discussion in the Bible. The Bible is not that kind of book. How, for example, can such freedom be reconciled with God's providential ordering of the Universe? and how can the paradox be maintained that bestowal of divine grace is the condition of human freedom? Why is it that man so often uses his freedom to defy God and, temporarily, to frustrate His purposes?

The Garden of Eden myth shows the introduction of a rebellious will into the affairs of God and of men. Whether the fall, there depicted, ought to be interpreted psychologically as a "fall upwards", the arrival of spiritual self-consciousness in man, is a moot point. True the myth provides no answer to the question as to why men should so often "miss the mark", and sin. There is mystery here, and no explanation has so far been offered which is rationally acceptable. Nor does the conception of a cosmic catastrophe either within history or (as Origen suggests) before history which infected man's posterity: nor resort to evolutionary categories which see sin as an anachronism, as the survival of the primitive in more developed man— neither of these helps very much with the theoretical problem. The rabbinic teaching on the Yetzer Hara and the Yetzer Hatov—the good and the evil inclination—both implanted by God in man, so that out of the struggle a real virtue might be born, is interesting, but of course merely descriptive.

As it is, the Bible is not particularly concerned with the cause:

it is the fact of sin and the cure of sin which are its prime concern, since "there is no man that sinneth not". The tragedy of
sin is that it separates: it is destructive and anarchical. It prevents
a man from realising his end.

What is obviously true is that God has not elected to make
man "ready made". The Bible is close to everyday experience
when it depicts him in a state of becoming. He must submit to
living, learn through his mistakes, if he is purposely to grow
into maturity. Growth is perhaps the operative word and growth
means struggle. As to the outcome of the struggle, the Bible is
realistically optimistic, steering a steady middle course between
a naïve perfectionism and a cynical pessimism. The Bible
recognises that man is made in the image of God and for relationship with God—not absorption into Him: but that, in the
realisation of this potential glory, he is often "sore let and
hindered in running the race that is set before him." He
encounters a resistance in the will, which must be overcome
through Divine Grace and human effort. Progress is by no
means automatic. Often it seems as if there is a bias to evil; a
weakness in the will. Yet all this adds up to the fact that the
Bible shows man as personal, free, and accountable. The
Christian ethic must treat him in this full context.

The above reference to growth as an "operative word"
serves to introduce the last Biblical insight which is peculiarly
relevant to our subject; I mean the reality which it gives to
"history", to the time process. Without such reality, what has
been said above of man as a free and responsible person, capable
of effective development, would lack any real meaning. It is
significant (as has already been pointed out) that the East has no
philosophy of history nor does it envisage a purpose being worked
out through it. History is too particular, too changing, too
formless and chaotic to provide a real knowledge.

The Bible, however, accepts space-time as a real dimension,

and recognises that worthwhile "events" happen within it—and because of it. Space-time is necessary for development. As year succeeds year, the creatively new does not simply emerge: it happens. Something is being wrought out, is being fought out, is being won, through the succession of years. Men (and nations) grow into maturity, not by contracting out of time or turning their backs on the challenges it offers, but by entering into the manifold experiences which existential[1] living alone makes possible. In this respect, the future is unpredictable: for into it go the free choices which men make and God's own reaction to them.

There is a Christian doctrine which seems to go so far as to suggest that Ultimate Reality is itself enriched by its participation in time, a view different indeed from Professor Alexander's evolving Deity, but still difficult to comprehend.

I refer to the fact that orthodox theology asserts that when Jesus, the God-man, returned to the Father, he "took" with him that human nature which had been shaped and perfected through his earthly pilgrimage. I make no comment on this doctrine, the implications of which (it seems to me) have never been fully worked out: but that it should exist at all gives some idea as to the degree of reality which Christian Faith is prepared to give to that complex of human affairs—individual and collective—which for convenience we call history. Though it is only *in* men that the collective becomes self-conscious, yet societies, nations, civilisations, have their own separate existences and it is within both these contexts that God works.

The Christian sees his own pilgrimage within this history not as a process of degeneration till the metabolism of the body ceases to function: but as a process leading to fuller life. For this

---

[1] I use the word existential to mean committing oneself actively to life and experience in the present.

to happen, not withdrawal from time, but more intense penetration into time, is necessary, and this means entering into "group experiences".

At the "end" of history, for man and for nations, there is a kingdom, a consummation, when God and those who have striven to do His will, shall be vindicated and He shall reign. Time is not an unfortunate accident: it is a God-given dimension.

Reference to consummation and vindication is a reminder that, according to a full Biblical testimony, man's destiny is not confined to this particular terrestrial scene which he at present inhabits. There is a kingdom beyond it into which he enters. This fact has great ethical implications. In certain situations it may effect the nature of an ethical judgement, and the resolution with which a Christian commits himself to it. An Athanasius "contra mundum" may be encouraged the more firmly to take his minority view by the conviction that eternity is on his side. If our ambition is to "see life steadily and to see it whole", it is only realistic to take account of this more distant horizon. That such a transcendental historicism may be abused is evident from the eighteenth century, when a system of rewards and punishments debased morality to the level of a private insurance policy. I cannot in this respect refrain from quoting part of a sermon preached by Bishop Thomas Sherlock (1678–1761) to the Benchers of the Inner Temple:

"There can be no ground of foundation to persuade men to renounce the pleasures of this life and to expose themselves to the troubles and inconveniences which often are the companions of virtue and holiness in hopes of future glory and happiness, unless this future glory and happiness are so great and valuable as to recompense all the losses and sufferings which man must sustain in the pursuit of them. . . . (But) should religion at last prove a mere deceit, we know the worst of it: it is an error for which we cannot suffer after death. Nor will the infidels there have the pleasure to reproach us with our mistakes: they and we in equal rest shall sleep the sleep of death."

It is sad to see religion so depraved and Christian ethics dragged through the mire. But the abuse of a thing does not make it useless and this presentation is a travesty of the Christian view.

It remains true, however, that the long perspective against which Christian Faith sees the life of man is bound at times to affect how he may act. At least it must mean that when assessing the consequences of human action, he cannot leave this final hope out of account. "If in this world only we have hope", wrote St. Paul, "we are of all men most miserable": and Joseph Butler, in his famous Analogy of Religion, maintained, with great skill, that this present life gives every indication of being a preparation for another. In spite of the cogency of Sir Leslie Stephen's severe critique of this latter thesis, something in the argument remains.

This chapter arose out of the preceding one because it was suggested that certain distinctive elements in Western civilisation had their origin, in part, in certain distinctive features of the Christian Faith. The result of our somewhat cursory enquiry into the Biblical picture of man may be summarised under four headings.

(1) That God created all things *ex nihilo* and by an act of will. This has the effect of making possible the consecration of man's total experience; and also prompts him to scientific investigation.

(2) That the personal is an ultimate category, a conviction which has led to the birth of the democratic ideal.

(3) That the individual person realises himself within the group. Society as a whole needs to be redeemed as well as the individual.

(4) That the space-time continuum is, for both God and man, a real dimension, within which a dynamic history moves towards its "end".

A Christian ethic must safeguard and express these truths.

CHAPTER IV

THE ETHICS OF JESUS

In the preceding chapter, we have suggested the framework within which a Christian ethic must be fitted. It must respect people in their particularity, and be intensely personalistic: it must seek to promote growth and development: it must encourage the exploration and consecration of the whole territory of human experience: it must give significance to the life of the community, and see a divine purpose working itself out in history.

If such constitutes the framework, it is Jesus of Nazareth who for Christian Faith fills out the picture and it is to Jesus that we now turn .

Jesus, the word made flesh, the image of the Invisible God, holds a unique place in Christianity and by so doing makes Christianity unique. His status is far different from that of the Buddha in Buddhism or Plato in Platonism. If it could be proved that the Buddha never lived, but that a group of profoundly spiritual men later projected on to him, as an ideal or archetypal figure, what they believed to be true about human life, Buddhism would not finally be any the poorer; nor would its influence be seriously weakened. The same is not true of Christianity, for without a real and historic Jesus its moral dynamic would lose its strength; and it is inconceivable that without him, as a historic figure, the Faith would have succeeded in establishing itself in the amorphous religious environment of the Roman Empire. The emphasis of Christianity on "particularity" would lack an effective ground, and its moral witness would lose its cutting edge, if it were Christ-less.

Christianity draws its ethical power from the fact that Jesus was "in all things tempted like as we are, apart from sin"; and that as a subject of Imperial Rome, sharing this "too, too solid flesh", he identified himself with the will of God. It was not that he incarnated this will in terms of abstract principles: rather in meeting given situations as they came he committed Himself to God as He lived existentially in response to them. He did not therefore proclaim a moralism which can be reduced to precise form: but showed a life which to the Christian has unique value. For this reason, the ambition of his followers is not so much to be morally good as to be Christ-like; not to obey every jot and tittle of a formal law, but to realise, in and through committment to him, the joyful fruits of liberated living. The end of human life is thus beyond morality, and this end is seen in Jesus who not only manifests God but reveals man to himself. Thus St. Paul, when trying to persuade men into a true humility, is content to say: "Let that mind be in you, which was also in Christ Jesus". And the unknown author of "The Little Flowers of St. Francis" pays his highest compliment when he says of his master that "in all the acts of his life he was conformed to the life of that Blessed Christ".

But what is that life and that mind? Most Christians, I believe, would agree that Jesus displayed a unique moral insight into God's Will for men: though having said this they would find that their difficulty came in analysing this insight for the purpose of statement, without in so doing converting it into a propositional[1] system.

It is easy to ask the wrong kind of question of this ethic of Jesus, as, for example, whether he gave priority to the four cardinal Platonic virtues—wisdom, courage, orderliness and uprightness. This analytic approach will never get to the heart

[1] By propositional I mean expressed in terms of positive regulations and commandments.

of what Christian ethics are about. For a juster appreciation we must turn to the 'event' of Jesus and see his teaching within this context. The reader of the Gospels is made vividly aware of a challenging Christ: and it is the total impact which Christ makes upon him which is the stimulus of his response to it. You cannot assess a Bach Fugue (or respond to it) merely by cutting it up into bits.

The key to an understanding of the mind and the commitment of Jesus undoubtedly lies in his conception of the Kingdom of God, and in his own relationship to it possibly through seeing himself as the Suffering Servant of Second Isaiah—that sublime figure (be it individual or dedicated nation) who is to bring it about.

The nature of this Kingdom and the ethics which belong to it, we shall consider later. Its supreme significance, however, makes it important to enquire how Jesus set out to establish it, since "the same arts that doth gain a power must that power maintain". In brief, Jesus dedicated himself through a sacrificial self-giving which culminated in a Cross. In this Cross, the Christian sees not defeat but victory, not weakness but strength, not a scaffold but a throne. It is certainly a strange paradox of history that an emblem of shame and subjection, from which, so Cicero advises, the Roman must avert his gaze, has been seized upon by the Christian to become the hallowed symbol of a world-conquering faith. Jesus on a Cross is no stoic accepting, in passive if courageous resignation, a grim fate: but a disciplined and active Son abandoning himself to the Father's Will in order to build a Kingdom. As such, his self-giving represents an intuitive awareness of the basic structure of reality itself, and of the nature of effective spiritual power. In supremely identifying himself with the Will of God, sacrificially throughout life, and significantly on Calvary, Jesus in the last crisis of his Messianic destiny, realises finally in action what he had often laid down as normative of the fulfilled life.

Whether Jesus conceived his crucifixion as leading immediately to the Kingdom in its full splendour is not significant for our present purpose. I myself am inclined to think that Calvary moved more in the intimate and personal world of final committal; and that Jesus was sustained by a filial trust rather than a prophetic pre-vision of the precise shape of things to come, that is a blueprint of the mechanics of salvation. The grandeur of sacrificial self-giving is the trust that inspires it, rather than the consequences which necessarily flow from it. The certainty of assured results is often anathema or irrelevant to the highest dedication of love. The Kingdom can only be won the way of Jesus, since final Reality is self-giving. Jesus leaves the outcome of his dedication in the hands of God, in the sureness of faith, but not with the same kind of certainty as in mathematics or logic, that He will use it to usher in the Kingdom.

As Jesus sought to establish the Kingdom of God in this sacrificial way, so the ethical pattern for his followers is an ethic of love: but love in Jesus (within the framework of the Old Testament dynamic) has a high activist and personalistic content: and cannot be separated from his whole Jewish background. In Jesus, there is undoubtedly a concentration around this theme, which gives a qualitatively new significance to the Greek word ἀγαπη, and which makes it different from love as Plato, for example, understood it. Its particular and compulsive character may be seen in the following extract from the Sermon on the Mount:

"Ye have heard that it hath been said, an eye for an eye, and a tooth for a tooth: But I say unto you, That ye resist not evil: But whosoever shall smite thee on thy right cheek, turn to him the other also. And if any man will sue thee at law, and take away thy coat, Let him have thy cloak also. And whosoever shall compel thee to go a mile, go with him twain. Give to him that asketh thee, and from him that would borrow of thee, turn not thou away. Ye have heard that it hath been said, Thou shalt love thy neighbour and hate thy enemy, But I say unto you, Love your enemies, bless them that curse you, do good to them that hate you, and pray for them which despitefully use you, and persecute you. That ye may be the children of your Father which is in Heaven: For he maketh His sun to rise on the evil and on the good and sendeth rain on the just and on the unjust."[1]

Thus it is that Klausner, though maintaining in one part of his "Life of Jesus" that there is "not one item of ethical teaching which cannot be paralleled in either the Old Testament, the Apocrypha, or in the Talmudic and Midrashic literature of the period near to the time of Jesus"; yet later admits that in Jesus all is stamped "with the same peculiar hallmark". And this "hallmark" makes it plain that the fulfilled life is in essence self-giving. Like the grain of wheat it dies (seemingly) in order the greater to live. A life of this kind is one of obedience to God's Will: of cross-bearing: of loving one's enemies and experiencing persecution in the process; of profound humility and compassion: of commitment in the faith that moves mountains: of a concern for others which demands everything and is sensitive to their particularity: of an abandon which is prepared to trust in God's providence.

There can, I think, be little question, if the Gospels be taken as our source book, that the call of Jesus to his followers was to be heroic. His challenge was stern and uncompromising: and it was so, just because the high regard in which he holds people as children of God, made in His image, would not allow him to treat them at a less exalted level. It is as fellow builders of the Kingdom that he invites his disciples to be his "friends": and it is membership in a sacrificial community which he offers as reward. The ethics of the Kingdom, he says bluntly, are not

[1] Matthew V, 38–44.

those which obtain in the world—that is in society so far as it is organised independently of God. "Ye know that the Princes of the Gentiles exercise dominion over them, And they that are great exercise authority upon them. But it shall not be so among you: But whosoever will be great among you, let him be your minister: And whosoever will be chief among you, let him be your servant: Even as the Son of Man came not to be ministered into, but to minister and to give His life a ransom for many."[1]

In this sense (and it is important to recognise the limitation implied in this phrase) Jesus called his followers *out* of the world. He did not hesitate to accept the responsibility of sending them forth as sheep among wolves, a little flock which was to inherit the Kingdom. As they went, they must hunger and thirst after righteousness, be peacemakers, be merciful, be meek, even to loving their enemies. Such a pattern of conduct represented the supreme excellence of the Kingdom, lifting those who accept God's way into a higher order: it is not the quietism of withdrawal, but the activism of a dedicated personalism.

Yet there need be nothing dramatic about entering the Kingdom, for in some sense it is equivalent to a new birth, to being raised to the fullness of life even when one is old. Entering the Kingdom, with its absolute demand, can be as secret and simple as the silent growth of a grain of mustard seed, the giving a cup of cold water in the name of Jesus, or the casting a mite into the treasury. To enter the Kingdom means to change the motivation of human conduct from an external compulsion of fear to an inner constraint of love: to move away from praying in the market place to be seen of men (that is "to do good" or to "acquire merit") to a glad and joyful expression of filial gratitude and trust. Jesus saw even his works of healing as "signs"; signs of the breaking through of the Kingdom of God, whereby there came liberation for the tortured bodies of men as well as release

[1] Matthew xx, 25–28.

for their souls. His offering of forgiveness, likewise, brought freedom, for there can be no slavery more complete, nor any cancerous growth more insidious, than that which results from a deep sense of guilt, corrupting the heart. Indeed, Jesus saw men, who were uniquely equipped to enter God's Kingdom, oppressed and held in chains by the forces of evil. They were not free (or freed) and he came to liberate them by fighting total war against Satan. Men were the captives of sin, and sin in whatever form it may manifest itself comes from an inordinate self-love—from the desire to acquire, to oppress, to use every other "existent" as a means to one's own introverted ends. Inordinate self-love is rebellion against God, a missing of the mark, isolation and finally death. The mission of Jesus therefore was "to preach the gospel to the poor, to heal the broken-hearted, to preach deliverance to the captive, a recovering of sight to the blind, to set at liberty them that are bruised, to preach the acceptable year of the Lord".

Nor did Jesus, in this great ministry of reconciliation—for sin separates from God—see himself as plucking separate brands from the burning. Life in the Kingdom is social through and through. Sacrifice and renunciation demand "the other": love necessarily begets a community. It was to a "little flock" that the Kingdom was entrusted, since the Jews as a nation would not come into it.

The Sermon on the Mount (doubtless a collection of his sayings) constitutes the corporate ethics of the Kingdom. They are the law for the new Israel, more imaginative, more costly in self-giving, more spontaneous, more liberating than that of the old. Jesus sees himself as the servant, appointed and destined to establish the Kingdom: the historic figure who is to give to history (and within history) that new dynamic or momentum which is to move it towards its appointed "End". In doing this he is no anarchist destroying the law, but a disciplined son who fulfills the law through penetrating to its essential purpose.

It will be necessary, later, to discuss how relevant are the ethics of Christ's Kingdom to modern society and how different theologians have regarded them. There cannot, however (it seems to me), be any doubt as to what these ethics of the Kingdom were as Jesus himself understood and proclaimed them—or at least as the early Christian community thought him to have proclaimed them. In fact, this teaching has the individual ring of spiritual genius about it: and there is about it the unity, not of logical coherence but such as a living person might well give to it. The work, say of Shelley, is certainly diverse: but it bears the imprint of a particular mind. In the same way there is sharp individuality running throughout the teaching of Jesus. It is all in character, and there is no need to be concerned overmuch if some of it derives from the community he created. There must have been sufficient of his authentic sayings for them to build upon. The plain fact of the matter is that simple and un-complicated people (there are such!) when they read the New Testament do come away with a vivid and recognisable portrait in their mind; and they find what they read challenging, often "hard", but never incomprehensible. To some, indeed, the ethics seem so absolute as to demand the impossible and un-attainable; so perfectionist as to be almost irrelevant. But all find something distinctive in them.

It will be the task of the remainder of this book to see how this distinctive ethic fared when a new community, entrusted with the rich treasures of the Kingdom, sprang up around the name of Jesus.

It remains only to state, in this chapter, that to the believer, in view of the status of Jesus in the Faith, these ethics have more than a merely human authority behind them The Christian sees them as rooted in the final structure of spiritual reality itself—that is in God. The ethics of the Kingdom are a personal ethic because the personal is a final category in God. They are an ethic of love because love is the energising activity which makes of the trinitarian nature of God one Ground. They are sacrificial because within the Being of God, the Father-Son relationship involves sacrifice as a necessary ingredient within the experience of God. They are an ethic of obedience because they are an ethic of Sonship, and subordination and obedience are expressive of the relationship of Father to Son within God's own Being. They are a social ethic because Father, Son and Holy Spirit constitute the Ground of the fulfilled life of God. They are a dynamic ethic because God has given reality to the space-time continuum which He created and into which He entered, through incarnation, in a unique way.

It is the distinctively Christ-like commitment, grafted on to, or as some would say, growing out of the Hebraic historicism which for succeeding generations of Christians has constituted the dilemma.

III: MAINLY HISTORICAL

CHAPTER V

THE DILEMMA OF THE KINGDOM

THE EARLIEST PROFESSION of Christian belief was indeed simple, for it consisted solely of the affirmation "Jesus is Lord". Around this dedication, those called into fellowship in the name of Jesus lived their life. To be a Christian meant committal, the kind of committal to which Jesus had given himself throughout his own ministry and which culminated on Calvary. The early Apostles preached Jesus, and it was therefore natural that at first they should need to be eye-witnesses. By vivid narration, made the more powerful by the witness of a continuing community, they conjured up before those who were prepared to listen the picture of their living Lord. The rationale of this early evangel was equally simple: Jesus is Lord; join his community; live in his power the higher life of God's Kingdom —and await his return.

For the converted, committal to Jesus meant incorporation into the "ekklesia": and the consequent showing forth a Christ-like virtue. That there was something distinctively ethical in being a Christian no one doubted. The follower of Jesus certainly was called, in St. Paul's words, "to reflect as in a mirror the glory of the Lord".

In emphasising the challenge of commitment to Jesus as essentially involved in the first proclamation of the Gospel, it is worth noting that the same challenge has remained integral to the Gospel ever since. Encounter with Jesus, and consequent obedience, are essential to a pattern of Christian discipleship and no treatment of Christian ethics can fail to take account of them. George Bernard Shaw, in typically racy language which so often conceals his intense seriousness, comments in the preface to *Androcles and the Lion*: "We have always had a curious feeling that though we crucified Christ on a stick, he somehow managed to get hold of the right end of it, and that if we were better men we might try his plan."

Yet these early Christians might well have encountered an initial difficulty in their endeavour to take Christ seriously as a moral guide and example—that is to "try his plan". To appreciate this we must remember that as Jews they inherited a number of traditions not all of them easily brought into relationship with each other or capable, at the moment, of being realised through their Christian Faith. In their Jewish past, they had been taught a concern for the well-being of the community equally with the individual person: they recognised the place of law as given by God, and the need for social justice. But Jesus, in fulfilling the law, had lifted ethics into a new spiritual dimension: a new dimension of love and sacrifice; and he had died in order to do this. But how could these early Christians live sacrificially in the world and yet continue to inhabit it? Might it not be said of Jesus that it was his virtue in a hostile environment which had caused his death: and also that, as the unique servant of God, he had a specialised vocation? Was it really possible to display the distinctive fruits of the Kingdom in an alien land? The ambiguous situation to which such questions bear witness might well persuade Christians that the only way out of the dilemma was to turn one's back on the world: yet such a solution was in fact no solution, for the very nature of the Hebraic-Christian ideology pointed in exactly the other direction.

The problem, at the outset, was however not so urgent, and this for two reasons. First, because of the hourly expectancy of Christ's return, with the assumption that the historic order was soon to be wound up. Secondly, because Christians were busily concentrating their religious lives within their own communities

—"cells" which stood over against and were, in that sense, withdrawn from the world. Such communities arose inevitably from the organic emphasis which Jesus, as a Jew, had inherited from the old Israel.

It was unthinkable that Christians should be separated and isolated individuals, practising in seclusion a private pietism, each one in his own small corner. The Faith was as social in its implications as were the virtues which Jesus preached. Religion to Christians is relationship. In committing themselves to Jesus, the newly baptised necessarily committed themselves to one another. They became members of a compact and closely knit society: and the fact that many of them were recruited from the socially depressed classes made their sense of "belonging" to the new Israel more intense and absorbing. It was *within* these "cells" that the higher ethic of the Kingdom of God was to be lived out: and from them that Christians were to go out into the world. "The Church of Christ is the community where the Christian ethic is given by God and lived out in practice as an actual reality". In the first flush of enthusiasm, so we read in the Acts of the Apostles, "the multitude of them that believed were of one heart and of one soul: neither said any of them that ought of the things which he possessed was his own: but they had all things common".[1]

It was a splendid gesture, pointing not only to a strong sense of brotherhood but also to a recognition of the *absolute* demands which Christ made upon them as members of his Kingdom. True, this primitive communism did not last long, but that it should ever have existed is significant. Paul regarded the churches which he founded throughout the Romano-Greek world as the living embodiment of the Kingdom, in which people lived not after the "flesh" but after the "spirit". The fruits of the spirit, he wrote to Christians in Galatia, are "love, joy,

[1] Acts v, 32.

peace, long-suffering, gentleness, goodness, faithfulness, meekness, temperance." To the Church of Corinth he spoke of a "more excellent way", and composed for its encouragement his famous poem on love, which is none other (it has been often suggested) than a portrait of Jesus. In these early Christian communities, differences of race, of colour, of social class, were transcended.

The emphasis placed by the author of the Johannine Epistles on "love of the brethren", and by James on a down-to-earth goodness, make plain the comprehensive nature of the higher virtue to which the Christian was called.

In actual fact, as may be suspected, this ethical ideal, though consistently proclaimed, was not in practice realised. The letters of Paul reveal, only too plainly, his bitter disappointment, and indeed frustration, at the grievous divide between ambition and achievement. The reasons for this failure need to be stated because they bear upon much which is to follow.

First, of course, it was due to weak, sinful human nature—all too often a "given" upon which idealism can too easily shipwreck. It was not so much that these early Christians repudiated the new ethic as that in practice they did not live up to it. Clashes of temperament, due to the rich racial and social diversity in these early communities, often led to unhappy personal relations. A great deal of St. Paul's practical advice is therefore devoted to the right handling of personal relationships —a subject on which he shows extraordinary sensitivity and delicacy of feeling. But the fact that the early Christians fell short is a reminder that the ethical problem is not only one of knowledge but also one of power.

Secondly, it was found, in practice, to be quite impossible to seal off these Christian communities from the pagan world around them. Some followers of Jesus still had pagan husbands, wives or parents. Most of them had to work for their livelihood in the world, and in this capacity, if in no other, they occupied a niche in Roman society. Here lay the germ of much subsequent trouble. What was the relatiosnhip of the new ethic to the world outside? Was the ethic relevant?

The problem was—and still is, though it appears now in a different form—a crucial one. St. Paul's obvious way of tackling it was to try to make the Christian communities as self-sufficient as possible, looking outwards only to one another. These "cells" provided a social milieu, a body, in which Christian graces could grow and a distinctive Christian virtue flourish. Paul's constant endeavour was to persuade Christians not to resort to Roman courts to settle internal disputes, no matter how grave the provocation. To do so would blur the distinction between the Church and the world, and thus lead to a lowering of standards. Yet, on the other hand, by reason of his Jewish background, with its teaching on law, Paul could hardly fail to respect (and he did not fail to say so) the mighty Roman achievement in establishing order over a vast area, though its methods were hardly those of the Kingdom. He was proud of his Roman citizenship.

Thus in some respects Paul's attitude was ambiguous when it came to the relations between these early churches with their distinctive ethics and society around them. The fact is that there was no real need, so early, to think the matter through, and Paul was probably not clear in his own mind as to how the one related to the other. It is unreasonable to expect any man today to answer tomorrow's problems. Paul had no hesitation in commanding slaves to obey their masters, not simply because they had to, but in a spirit of Christian humility and service: their status gave them an opportunity to live sacrificially. His attitude to civic responsibility is passive rather than active, as the following quotation illustrates:

"Let every soul be subject unto the higher powers for there is no power but of God: the powers that be are ordained of God.

Whosoever therefore resisteth the power, resisteth the ordinance of God: and they that resist shall receive to themselves judgement. For rulers are not a terror to good works but to the evil. Wilt thou not then be afraid of the power? Do that which is good, and thou shalt have praise of the same: for he is the Minister of God to thee for good. But if thou do that which is evil, be afraid; for he beareth not the sword in vain: for he is the Minister of God, a revenger to execute wrath on them that doeth evil. Therefore ye must needs be subject not only for wrath but also for conscience sake. For this cause pay ye tribute also; for they are God's ministers, attending continually upon this very thing. Render therefore to all their due; tribute to whom tribute is due, custom to whom custom, fear to whom fear, honour to whom honour."[1]

This is indeed a most interesting passage, though it is perhaps a mistake to read too much into it. The fact that Caesar exercises a coercive jurisdiction and is a "revenger executing wrath" does not prevent him from being a minister of God, i.e. used by God, and the Christian must submit, for this jurisdiction represents an overall attempt to realise a rough justice. What St. Paul does not have to face up to is the attitude of the Christian who finds himself in such a position of responsibility. The Christian "cells", during his lifetime, were tiny and their membership uninfluential. It would be extremely unlikely that any Christian so early would hold responsible office under the government, though we do read the enigmatic phrase: "they of Caesar's household" (probably slaves) and Luke later addresses his Gospel to the "most excellent Theophilus". But it is clear that Paul never had to concern himself with a Christian foreign policy for the Roman Empire, or to ask himself what it meant to live sacrificially in the day to day discharge of government. He had more than he could do to bring these infant churches into the

[1] Romans xiii, 1-7.

Kingdom: to have attempted to bring secular government within it as well would have seemed, even to his sanguine and dauntless spirit, an impossible ambition—though, in another and much more personal context, he had to wrestle within himself with the seeming antithesis of "law" and "grace".

What St. Paul set out to do was to encourage the first believers to live their lives in simple discipleship of Jesus, growing in grace within the Christian community where effective personal relationships were possible. In the world they would "take" what came to them, discharging their duties for conscience sake, and in their (usually) subordinate capacities remembering that Christ, their master, though equal with God, "humbled himself, and took upon him the form of a servant".

But if Paul did not find it necessary to go further in working out a relationship between the Church and the world, it was yet he, more than any other man, who suggested in more immediate and personal terms what discipleship of Jesus ought to be. By so doing, he converted "goodness" from obedience to a legalistic code into the joyful expression of a filial trust in God.

The results of this insight into the nature of Christian ethics have been tremendous. The tragedy of moralism (in whoever professes it) is that it leads to strain, frustration, and often to a self-destroying pride. The effort to win "salvation" (that is spiritual wholeness) by successful achievement leads paradoxically to inversion, and in the highly sensitive moralist, to neurotic frenzy. Paul (for he had tried it) came to recognise the sterility of such an attempt (though he is never quite certain as to how far the psychological condition of frustration might not prove a preparation for the gospel). Striving to obey the Jewish law, he had made goodness cheese-paring, niggardly, and precise; the cult of mere duty; the painful effort, not primarily to help others, but to become good *through* helping them. The paradox of this kind of endeavour is that "the other" merely becomes a means to the securing of our own moralistic ends. What in fact ought to encourage escape from the prison house of the self, serves only to lock the door more firmly. That which should lead to liberty becomes a bondage. Such virtue is unlovely, unattractive, rigid and unyielding: it is the goodness that can be evil spoken of.

St. Paul was himself rescued from an introverted moralism, a quite literally soul-destroying personal situation, by the experience of encounter with Christ and all that flowed from it—the grateful acceptance that God was as Jesus revealed him, the Father: and that what was required of him (Paul) was not a moral blitz against God, an aggression against ultimate Reality in order to justify himself, but rather a committal in faith to Jesus. Indeed, it is by faith that the just live and it is out of gratitude for experienced succour that the fruits of the spirit grow—love, joy and peace in believing. The effect is to make ethical behaviour a by-product. The good man sheds anxiety; he ceases to worry about his goodness and experiences the truth of what Augustine meant when he wrote (though he did not always himself live up to it): "Love God and do what you like". Right behaviour, though losing none of its claim, is seen to be something which you cannot aim to achieve directly. For this reason, the moral ideal of Christianity is far different from the calm resignation of stoicism: and finds its fulfilment in following a person (Jesus) and not in cultivating a certain state of mind. This gives to it its dynamic. It is in this respect not irrelevant to Paul's ethical view to notice how intimate he regards this relationship with Jesus to be. "I live yet not I but Christ liveth in me", he writes; and again: "I bear in my body the marks of the Lord Jesus"—a suggestive phrase which may refer to something analogous to the stigmata. Certainly it has a reference to sacrificial living

So it comes about that Christianity, in its highest form of expression, is non-legalistic. It places the final emphasis on fulfilled personal living: on grace rather than effort: on faith rather than works. This does not mean, of course, that a man must run before he can walk, or that there is no need for self-discipline. The difficulty in stating the Christian ethical view is that the *whole* of it needs to be stated *all* the time. Paul, at least in some of his moods, was grateful for the law, the cult of achievement. It pointed to a high ethical standard: and through his very inability to live up to it, he was made aware of a more ultimate personal need—the need to be loved. Hence, ethical behaviour, to Paul and to every Christian, reflects a grateful response to God, who is the Father, for mercies freely given. Christian virtue, therefore, activist as it is, has about it something of the effortless ease of a great work of art: and as it is expressed in uniquely particular persons, every expression of it is unique. Into a work of art there doubtless go the mastery of a technique and great self-discipline—but, finally, the artist is free of these things, and, while not forgetting what they have taught him, revels in a greater liberty. As the artist must "see" before he can create, and such creation is a necessary fulfilment of the total experience, so the Christian must "know" (experience) before a Christian virtue can be realised.

(II)

It is necessary, at this point, to return to our earlier consideration, namely, the difficulty which the first Christians would have felt had they endeavoured to relate their distinctive Christian dedication to life in the wider society. As to this problem, it must be confessed that Jesus, like Paul, had little to say. He refused to be drawn into the political discussions of the day, and avoided being involved in the controversy with Rome. His immediate concern was with the Kingdom and what happened within it. He left it to future generations (who must themselves live existentially) to wrestle with the problem of relating the

Kingdom to the world. Paul, in the communities which he founded, recognised the difficulty, but he was not called upon to do more than give a rather inconclusive answer to it as we saw a few pages earlier.

It is important, however, to take our somewhat sketchy historic survey a little further: since if Paul found it more or less possible (though by no means completely so) to seal off his Christian communities from the world, it became more and more difficult to do this as the years went on. Christianity grew: and with increasing numbers, more influential people began to enter the Christian fellowship or at least became interested. It is of the nature of most religions, however, to breed a conservative temper of mind (no matter how revolutionary their origin!) and Christianity proved to be no exception. The Christian Church tended to cling to its older, detached and disinterested attitude towards political affairs, the more so because its Faith remained an illegal one, and the psychology induced by spasmodic persecution cut deep. To become a permitted religion would have meant to accept the status of being one amongst many other religions—and this Christians just would not do.

The general position in which believers stood in their relations with the world during the first three centuries may be illustrated from their attitude towards military service. It is remarkable how scanty, and often inaccurate, is the attention given by Church historians to this not unimportant subject: and even such a well-informed and conscientious scholar as Dr. Bethune Baker (in his "The Influence of Christianity on War", 1888) hardly does justice to the *whole* of the evidence. The fact is that a majority of church members, at least up to about A.D. 250—and this was the period when the Church by its devoted virtue planted Christianity in the Roman world—maintained an orthodoxy of pacifism, and felt this to be quite essential to a full Christian witness. Apart (possibly) from the New Testament,

there is no positive evidence before A.D. 170 of any Christian, after his conversion, continuing to serve in the Roman army,
though it must be remembered, of course, that no Jew or slave
was eligible to join the legions. Nor is there any record of
prayers being offered for the armed forces until the time of
Tertullian. Indeed, very few Christians entered the service
of the government at all, or became magistrates—as such, they
would have had to pass sentence of death—before well on into
the third century, so that Lecky writes of this period that
Christian opinions "were usually formed without regard to the
necessities of civil or political life".

Among the most prominent exponents of this early pacifism
were Tertullian, Origen, Cyprian, Arnobius, Lactantius and
Hippolytus. It sprang principally from an absolute refusal to shed
blood; to indulge in violence of any kind; or to associate with
idolatry. Such practices, so early Christians believed, had been
categorically forbidden by Jesus, who had lived out a non-
violent, personalistic ethic. The strength with which many
adhered to what they regarded as the example of their Lord
may be seen in the number of men who, when converted in the
legions, suffered martyrdom rather than continue to serve.

The most mature apologia for this early Christian pacifism
was put forward by Origen (c. 185–254) in reply to an attack
made by the heathen philosopher Celsus, in his "True Dis-
course" written in A.D. 178. Celsus roundly condemned the
Christians for their unwillingness to accept service under the
government, and in particular their refusal to "fight as soldiers"
or to "share military command".

Origen, in his "Contra Celsum" (A.D. 248) admits quite
frankly that the charge is true. He writes: "To those who ask
us whence we have come or whom we have (for) a leader, we
say that we have come in accordance with the counsels of Jesus
to cut down our warlike and arrogant swords of argument into

ploughshares and to convert into sickles the spears we formerly used in fighting. For we no longer take sword against nation nor do we learn any more to make war, having become sons of peace for the sake of Jesus, who is our leader, instead of (following) the ancestral (customs) in which we were strangers to the covenants." "(Jesus) did not deem it becoming to his own divine legislation to allow the destruction of any man whatever".

Origen was perfectly aware that this absolute personalism, leading to pacifism, invited the comment from opponents "that if everybody followed this 'way' then the Emperor would be deserted and the Empire fall a prey to the barbarians." This objection is certainly understandable, for the Roman government was in fact busily engaged in policing the frontiers of the Empire, and thereby endeavouring to preserve inviolate a territory within which some measure of law and justice might be maintained.

Origen's reply is frank, realistic and particularly relevant to the question: "Is there a distinctive Christian ethic?" Indeed, what he says only makes sense if an affirmative answer is given, for he draws a distinction between what a conscientious pagan and an equally conscientious Christian might feel it right to do.

The Emperor, Origen writes, exercises a coercive jurisdiction internally in the administration of justice (torture and death) and externally in war. The Christian has a duty to pray for him and, if his cause is just, for his success in a military operation. It would be wrong, given the Emperor's principles, for him not to lead his armies and for his non-Christian subjects not to support him. Theologically, this means that God does not refrain from working within a system of power, and that in a world where so much moral relativity obtains, God prefers the lesser evil to the greater. But the Christian, in his relations with both God and man, is in a far different position from his pagan brother. He is called to be distinctively Christ-like, and he cannot, in the supposed interest of the state, compromise this particular loyalty

Taking a *long* view, the greatest contribution he can make to his fellow men is to be true to his distinctive commitment.

Origen's words have been translated into a more modern idiom by Dr. H. H. Farmer, who writes: "The Christian must seek to keep dominant in his mind the sense of his special vocation in Christ. He must seek to keep dominant in his mind his calling and ministry as a redeemed man who knows through Christ the real order in which God has set mankind, and is appointed to be himself, in the spirit of the Cross under God, at all times a reconciler and an agent of the Kingdom. This involves the principle that all other offices, callings, and responsibilities must for the Christian be subordinated to the one supreme vocation."

To quote a contemporary analogy, Origen might well argue that a war fought by the United Nations to secure justice was on a higher moral plane that that fought by a colonial power to preserve its dominion—yet the Christian may still feel that his specialised vocation as a member of Christ's flock forbids his taking part in it. God will use him in ways "more consonant with the unique insight and powers of the Gospel". Such a renunciation, Origen would have said, in fact did say, is *not* anti-social, because God can more effectively use this kind of dedication in order to build His Kingdom.

Had the Church remained true to Origen's convictions, one cannot help wondering whether the story of Christian Europe would have been quite so fratricidal in its strife. All that we can say is that God would have had a different situation within which to work.

The dilemma for the Christian was a real one, namely, how to fit his distinctive Faith, with its sacrificial, highly personal and non-violent ethics, into the duties of citizenship—that is, how to be faithful both to the Jewish and the "Jesus" inheritance. The tension was made the more acute because an incarnational Faith inevitably gave value to the maintenance of the social order. Yet as more people joined the Christian Church, so did the

c

intense loyalties, bred in the atmosphere of the small groups, tend to weaken. The latter point is important.

Early Christians were not particularly conscious of the state, for their interests and loyalties were elsewhere. True, the state was there in the background, necessary to preserve law and order. Both Paul and Peter were prepared to admit (as we have seen) that at a lower level (that is the enforced level of a coercive jurisdiction) it was doing a good work, as the Christian Church similarly, in its smaller groups and at the higher levels of freedom, grace and love, was doing a good work. The former constituted a coercive society, to maintain which the sword is not used in vain: the latter was a free, indeed a freed society, an "ekklesia", called out of the world to realise, in its corporate life, the "reign of God". But the points at which the one converged on the other were not clear nor the relationship between them defined when they became involved in each other's life.

Certainly, at least in practice, the Christian had to live in both. Did this mean a double standard—one standard for the world, another for the beloved community? The instincts of the early Christians led him to affirm that whatever it might mean, it could not mean this.

Thus it came about that the early Christian pacifism was ambiguous, because, along with the intuition of incompatibility between the ethics of the Kingdom and the violence of war, there went also a lack of a sense of real responsibility for the wider life of the Empire. It needs to be remembered, of course (in fairness to Christians), that the Roman state was not a democracy, and in its later years increasing power was concentrated in fewer and fewer hands. The sense of civic responsibility declined to an alarming extent (even among non-Christians) as the Empire became more monolithic, this being one among many factors undermining both the strength and the stability of the Roman Empire, since so few people had an effective stake in it. The slave, of course, to all practical purposes, had no legal or political rights, and many Christians were slaves. It was comparatively easy, therefore, for followers of Jesus to be indifferent to the fate of the Empire. If the barbarians stampeded across the frontiers, then, in Biblical terms, it was but one more example of the judgement of God; and as to wars and rumours of wars, had not the Master said that they would come?

Yet such detachment could not permanently exist unless Christianity either remained a very small, and politically, insignificant minority-group (in which case it would probably have finally disappeared altogether) or unless its believers were prepared to deny something very real in their inheritance. The minority tradition of withdrawal was not the only one which Christians had inherited. Earlier in this book, reference was made to the insistence by the Hebrew prophets on the need to dedicate the whole national life to the will of Yaweh. Social justice was essential to holiness, and a corrupt judicature an offence to the Most High. The Old Testament scriptures, the sacred books of the old Israel, became equally sacred to the new and (apart from the later conception of a righteous remnant) they bore witness to no minority group but to a nation which was called upon to serve God—a whole community whose total life must be lived as under the judgement of God Himself. Its law, its government, its economics, its foreign policy, its ritual observances, all were part (or ought to be a part) of one inter-related whole, a corporate endeavour to be a "holy nation". No distinction was made between the sacred and secular, or if made it soon withered away.

Every time the Old Testament scriptures were read in the primitive Church—and they were read regularly—the Christian was confronted, and challenged, by a historic situation when the nation-church, into whose inheritance he believed himself to have entered, played a far different rôle. He could not fail to notice the contrast: and may well have asked himself whether it was not due simply to a historic accident, to the failure of the old Israel as a nation to become the new. It was inevitable, therefore, that, from within its *own* thought-forms, the early minority psychology should be submitted to influences deriving from God's initiative in history, that is from His covenant with a nation.

The logic of events also helped to bring a change. As more and more converts were recruited from those who held, or were capable of holding, responsible civic office throughout the Empire, so was the gulf between the Christian community and the world willy-nilly being bridged. Problems which Paul had not needed to tackle became urgent and people wanted guidance. Thus the early pacifism increasingly became questioned. It was possible, of course, to maintain, as had Origen, that since the practice of warfare was contrary to the will of God, the Christian pacifist was a better citizen of Rome, since he was witnessing to a divine order, upon respect for which the Imperial welfare must finally depend. This is indeed a possible view, but it is easier for a minority group to maintain it. The fact is that a Church, whose membership was rapidly increasing, began to look outward and, in a new way, to face up to the realities of power; and to entertain a sense of responsibility for its overall use. Their incarnational faith, paradoxically, drove Christians to it, yet they were bound to recognise (even before Lord Acton!) how corrupting power can be, and that it can only be safely exercised when it is brought within an overall expression of love (that is why it is safely exercised so seldom).

Those who committed themselves to a faith nurtured in history (unlike Mithraism which was a psychological projection —"there never was a Mithras and he never slew a bull") could not escape finally being embroiled *in* history and to become makers of it. They were not only drawn in but driven in by the inner momentum of their own ideology.

Nor can it be doubted that the worsening position of the Empire both in the East and in the West, as the barbarians increased their pressure on the outposts, made the Christian position of detachment more difficult psychologically to maintain. The dilemma became even more acute when the question changed from whether the Christian had any stake in Roman civilisation to whether he had any stake in civilisation itself. Did it matter if the pattern of law and order, no matter how imperfect, which the government of Rome had painfully established, and was now struggling to preserve, were swept clean away? If the grand consummation of all things was beyond history, did this mean that civilisation itself was finally expendable? If it was important that civilisation should be preserved, how could the Christian help to ensure its preservation? Could he oppose the barbarians with his "distinctive virtues"?

The ultimate difficulty confronting Christians was this; how to ensure that, when they were drawn in, the contribution which they made to the shaping of events was veritably Christian; and that they were swinging secular history into the orbit of the Kingdom of God?

These questions have a strangely modern ring about them: and they became desperately urgent in the fourth century as the once mighty Roman Empire tottered to its fall. The relation of the Christian Church to this history was the theme of St. Augustine's *De Civitate Dei*: and what Christians as a body had finally to decide was whether their Faith could inspire, support and direct not only a religious and non-governmental group within a political order, but that political order itself. The question can be put another way. Could the ethical pattern to which Christianity was committed realise itself in (or accommodate itself to) the handling of power and the direction of the community life, as well as determine, as it undoubtedly could, the more intimate personal relations of Christian to Christian.

Questions of this kind are not answered by formal discussion but by what F. D. Maurice called "life and experiment". They are decided as men submit themselves to the stresses and strains of actual living, and are forced, sometimes in spite of themselves, to act. It will come as no surprise that the tendency within the Christian Church was on the whole steadily towards integration: to being the leaven working in the lump rather than a community called out of the world. The motives leading to this new attitude were mixed—a concern for the well-being of the wider world, as well as a lowering of standards which made for compromise. A pointer in this direction may be seen in the aftermath of the Decian persecution. During the fierceness of this attack on the Church, many Christians burnt the Scriptures and renounced the Faith. When the persecution ceased, many of those who had "lapsed" wished to be re-admitted. A fierce controversy broke out, but the Church finally decided to open its doors to these weaker brethren. By so doing it made plain that the Church was a community not only of the elect and the saved, but also of those in the process of being saved. But the real transformation was brought about by a political decision.

In the year 306 there ascended the throne of the Roman Empire Flavius Valerius Constantinus, who as Emperor was increasingly aware of the dangers confronting the Empire by invasion from without and by division and weakening morale from within. The Christian Church now constituted almost an "imperium in imperio", a dominion which successive Emperors had failed to break. Might not this vigorous and proselytising Faith, wedded to history in spite of itself, be the means of giving the Empire new life and support? Would it not be wiser to win the goodwill of these Christians, to make their faith a permitted religion and finally to establish it as the one religion of the Empire? Already the Church had a firmly entrenched episcopal system, which duplicated religiously the administrative divisions of the Empire. This fact alone had bred an increasing Christian concern for the stability of society and a greater respect for settled government. Particularly in the capital city of Rome had the status of its bishop risen with the fall in the status of the Emperor.

Thus in A.D. 313 the Emperor Constantine made the Christian Faith a permitted religion; and later it became the official faith of the Roman Empire.

The importance of these events is manifest, since they have shaped both the history of the Christian Church and the future of Western (and therefore world) civilisation. So far as Constantine was concerned, his policy was the clear recognition that Christianity (so far as he understood it) could be the religion of a great empire: that its ethical pattern was not incompatible with the exercise of political responsibility and the discharge of government: and that it was capable of breeding good citizens and capable rulers.

We must remember that the older pagan religions had been integrated by customary ritual acts with the pattern of everyday civic life. True they had come to lose their relevance, and intellectuals no longer believed in them as representing a true picture of reality: but at their best they had served to give dignity to society and some "mana" or "mystique" to government. Constantine never doubted that the Christian Faith was equally able to discharge this traditional function in society and to do it to better advantage.

How far Constantine, in coming to his political decision, was fully aware of the particular virtue for which Christianity stood is doubtful: he probably saw it as the most alive and virile faith in the Empire, encouraging a high personal integrity and strongly on the side of law and order.

On the part of the Christian Church, the willingness with which it was prepared to accept its new position is significant.

Such a decision (not a formal one of course) was the frank recognition that to be a group within society was not of the essence of the Church: and that there was nothing, as such, incompatible between citizenship in the Empire and discipleship of Jesus—though the rite of baptism must always mean that entry into the Christian Church was by "grace" and not "by nature".

The acceptance of Christianity as a state religion also implied that it was possible for an Emperor on a throne, whose business was government, and who as such was pledged to the keeping of the peace, and the policing of a vast territory—that is, one who is necessarily involved in the ambiguities of handling power—to accept Jesus as Lord. This was indeed a revolution, for it could only mean that the Christian must now formally accept responsibility for the society in which he lived, that is for the general direction of its life. The ethics of the Kingdom and the ethics of the world must be brought into relationship. New ethical problems were bound to result from this confrontation.

Some sensitive Christians in the fourth century frankly regarded this new status of their Faith with mixed feelings. They doubted whether the recognition of Christianity by Constantine had done as much to sanctify the state as it had done to secularise the Church. Certainly, when Christianity occupied the rôle of a state religion, new motives to adopt it increasingly began to operate. Membership of the Church became respectable, and many sought it for reasons which lacked deep spiritual conviction. The removal of the threat of persecution prevented fanatical Christians from indulging in a frenzy of masochism but it also removed a challenge to heroism. Some who felt the new "mood" acutely, and were painfully conscious of a lowering of standards, sought refuge in the pietism and uncomplicated holiness which solitude alone seemed to make possible—though it is interesting here to notice that so strong was the social urge in Christianity that the hermit soon gave way to the monk in a religious community.

Judgements on the processes of history (particularly for the Christian!) are always precarious. In spite of this, however, the opinion may be hazarded that the Church was right, recognising all the dangers which such a choice inevitably involved, in accepting the new status which Constantine was prepared to confer upon it. Nothing is more corrupting than power— nothing perhaps but a refusal to accept it when it can be used redemptively. Christianity has a lot to say about power, and believes that a corrective to its abuse is the readiness to admit that unregenerate man is likely to abuse it. A Christian Church which refused in A.D. 313 to accept the responsibility of facing up to the fact of power would have been a church which turned its back on the challenge confronting it at that hour—a church which refused to live existentially. There may, of course, be "tides in the affairs of men" when a Christian community might consider it right not to accept power and official status because of the "strings" attached to it. A.D. 313, I suspect, was not such a time.

The immediate results (ethically) flowing from the changed status of the Christian Church, so far as the state was concerned, were not spectacular. This is not surprising. There was no sudden breaking through of God's Kingdom, no sudden manifestation or outpouring of the fruits of the spirit. The social and political order is much too resistant for this to happen: and historians have not found it easy to decide what its precise effects were. Perhaps it may be fairly claimed that one result was (gradually) to make the vicious penal code a little more humane and merciful, and for the condition of some of the slaves to be a little improved. A more immediate result, however, can be seen in the official abandonment of the earlier pacifism, which had been tending to weaken for many years, and was never in fact universal.

It is quite clear that Constantine would never have contemplated adopting a religion which forbade his subjects to shed blood either judicially or in war: and during his reign it is hardly any exaggeration to say that the Church as a whole (the qualification is important) "definitely gave up her anti-militarist leanings, abandoned all her scruples, finally adopted the imperial point of view, and treated the ethical problem involved as a closed question". Indeed the sign of the Cross now became a military emblem, and the nails supposedly taken from it (and sent as a present to Constantine by his mother) were made into a bridle and helmet for the Emperor's use in time of war. In A.D. 314 the Council of Arles, though it did not go so far as to excommunicate Christian soldiers who by reason of their faith abandoned the army, at least left military service "perfectly free and open to Christians". Athanasius even went so far as to say that "to destroy enemies in war is lawful and worthy of praise". Both Ambrose of Milan and Augustine of Hippo concurred with this view, which even non-pacifist Christians of an earlier generation would have regarded as abhorrent.

The wheel had indeed turned full circle when in A.D. 416 under the Codex Theodosianus (XVI. x. 21) the army became a Christian prerogative and non-Christians were forbidden to enlist. Dean Milman comments: "For the first time the meek and peaceful Jesus became a god of battle, and the Cross, the Holy Sign of Christian redemption, a banner of bloody strife."

It would be inaccurate, however, to suppose that this "capitulation of the Church" as some have called it—Dr. G. J. Heering, the Scandinavian scholar, describes it as "the fall of Christianity"—was sudden or dramatic. It was not. "The Testament of our Lord", a Church Order compiled in Syria or South-East Asia Minor not earlier than the middle of the fourth century, forbids the baptism of soldiers unless they first renounce the army: and the same discipline is insisted upon, though in a less drastic form, in the Egyptian Church Order. A fitful witness to an earlier attitude was thus maintained throughout this century. Theognus of Phrygia was martyred for refusing to join the Legions; St. Martin of Tours suddenly withdrew from the army before a battle, offering to stand unarmed between the rival hosts; and St. Basil the Great gave it as his opinion that those who shed blood in war should abstain from Communion for three years.

This abandonment of a primitive pacifism is significant, quite independently of whatever assessment is made of it as a Christian attitude: and few will deny that something distinctive (and decisive) went out of Christian witness with its passing—and has never returned. It is a sobering reflection that a Church which at one period, at least where a majority of its members were concerned, took its stand against violence of any kind, forbade torture and the shedding of blood, even to the extent of encouraging martyrdom on behalf of these convictions, should at a later period in its history have initiated the barbarities of the Inquisition, have hounded witches to death amidst quite indescribable horrors (see Lecky!) and at an even later period in its history have found itself unable to condemn the dropping of the first nuclear bomb which blew to smithereens some 70,000 men, women and children.

It is the more sobering when it is remembered that Lactantius wrote in A.D. 305 of the Christian: "He regards it as wrong not only to inflict slaughter himself, but even to be present with those who inflict it."

That this pacifism was so decisively shed calls attention once more to the problem which consistently confronts us—the incompatibility which was felt to exist (by Christians themselves) between what seemed a distinctive and absolutist Christian ethic and the behaviour appropriate in a sinful and power ridden world. Many followers of Jesus in the fourth century who saw without regret the passing of this earlier pacifism (or were hardly aware of it) were yet conscious of the dangers inherent even in the opportunities which opened up under the new status conferred upon the Church. Christian teaching as to the lifelong nature of the marriage relationship and the sanctity of the home: on justice as the objective expression of God's will: on respect for rulers (up to a point): on the simple virtues and the accountability of all men, ruler and ruled, to the divine Judge—all these were obviously seen to be helpful to the morale of society and the stability of government. But a sacrifical ethic, expressive of an intense personalism, such as was the splendour of the Incarnate life of Jesus—it was not easy to see how this could be made relevant or effective outside the immediate territory of home and local Christian community. How in fact was it to be introduced into the more resistant context of state authority and governmental decree?

It will be the task of the next chapter to follow up this dilemma, which almost necessarily results from a very real ambiguity within Christianity itself, caused (as I believe) by the difficulty of bringing together the Hebraic emphasis on law and the community with the more personalistic and sacrificial ethic of Jesus.

On the one hand, Christianity is a historical religion, claiming to see "value" in events, and encouraging its believers, in their various capacities and functions, to commit themselves to citizenship. It has its roots far back in a theocracy, and understands God's purpose for men the better because of a particular Incarnational Act. It invites men to enter into as wide an experience of life as possible (since God's creative activity lies behind all things) and not to withdraw from experience in order to contemplate a static perfection.

On the other hand, Christianity places the sacrificial life of Jesus—a Cross—right in the centre of its theology, and sees there God most powerfully at work. Paul understood well the inherent paradox of Christian Faith when he frankly admitted that to the Greeks the Cross was "foolishness" and to the Jews a "stumbling block", though to them that believe, both Jews and Greeks, it was "the power of God unto salvation".

I recall a distinguished member of the original B.B.C. Brains Trust, during the last war, commenting that he thought it would be advisable, "for the duration", to forget the teaching of Jesus. It is not difficult to understand the scruples which lay behind the observation, and this was in part what actually happened. The cry "We'll give it 'em back" seems very far removed from the ethics of the Kingdom, and from the simple command "If thine enemy hunger, feed him, if he thirst, give him drink". Yet Christianity is the very religion which drives people *to* history, and demands that they play a decisive part in it!

The easiest way out of this challenging dilemma is, of course, either to forget it, or to deny that it exists—a state of self-deception which has had too many exponents throughout the long course of Christian history. Some followers of Jesus have felt that they could only solve it by retreating from the world and entering a separated religious community: or by accepting a mere passive citizenship, which in this department of life does what it is told and asks no questions. Others again, in endeavouring to face up to this dilemma, have dealt with it theologically in one of two ways, either by claiming that the high morality of Jesus can be lived out, by grace, in every sphere of human life, individual and collective, and that God somehow will make such a perfect dedication effective: or by asserting that the absolute ethics of Jesus are not meant for (i.e. in the nature of the case cannot be realised in) the life of the believer in *all* his capacities in the world.

Before discussing these various approaches, however, it will be helpful if our brief historical survey is taken a little further.

CHAPTER VI

A CHRISTIAN SOCIETY AND ITS BREAK-UP

THE COLLAPSE OF the Roman Empire did not prove the end of all things as some contemporaries had expected. A new civilisation painfully and slowly emerged out of it, as the barbarians, who proved remarkably suggestible, were first tamed and then educated.

The shape of this civilisation was largely conditioned by the practical necessities of the time—that is by social, economic, and political needs. It was no longer of any use for European man to look to a central government for protection or to expect Rome any more to enforce law and justice from Hadrian's Wall to the Danube. Whatever stability and governmental order the new social milieu was capable of providing must be organised locally—and this is essentially what feudalism during the Middle Ages (or the early years of it) was. Of course, the resulting political and economic systems varied from territory to territory according to local needs and whatever elements of Roman order survived, but in essence they represented a grouping together of people in small economic units, each person accepting a defined status (sometimes even of servitude) in return for such protection and security as was given him. Later theory gave to this system (or imposed upon it) the logical symmetry of a hierarchical pyramid from serf to emperor: but, basically, feudalism arose not out of logic but from an experienced need—the need for order over against chaos.

So far as the new pattern was concerned, the Christian Church did not enter late in the day (as it had in the Roman Empire) almost as a new boy or intruder: it was there in the beginning, and the barbarians showed a surprising readiness to learn from Rome and an equal readiness to embrace the Christian Faith. Certainly the Christian Church provided what the barbarians needed, and it was this Church which piloted over into the new age many of the values of Roman civilisation (and what it had borrowed from Greece) as well as the verities of its own Faith. During the Middle Ages it was the Christian Church which consecrated kingship: which held aloft an ethical ideal of justice: which provided the trained personnel (the civil service) essential to the discharge of government: and which surrounded citizenship with the dread sanctions of a supernatural religion. Thus the historian Green describes the English nation as "the child of the Church", so much did the latter condition the growth of the former.

For these reasons, many have regarded Mediaeval Europe (in theory at least) as a Christian society, in which a definite effort was made to organise, or at least to direct, the life of the community around a Christian ideology; and to establish a social pattern within which a Christian ethic could find visible expression. This may well appear a somewhat optimistic view, and certainly it is not true in any absolute sense: but the fact that the claim has been put forward must be of interest to us in our study of Christian ethics.

We have already noticed two things in respect of the society which arose out of the collapse of Rome. First, that its economic structure, as well as its governmental system, arose out of basic human needs when law and order broke down. Secondly, that the Christian Church, working within this total situation, and being itself part of it, attempted to control, to direct, and to consecrate it. The fact that the Church stood for an order of civilisation helped to prevent a "failure of nerve" at a critical time when courage and hope were desperately needed to build again. There were few scruples now as to whether the Christian Church ought to enter the social and political order. If it had

not done so, it is doubtful whether its own ordered and worshipful life would have been allowed to continue.

As it was, a systematic theological statement covering the
whole territory of man's earthly life and deriving substance,
as was thought, from Christian doctrine, was patiently worked
out by mediaeval theologians. The exponents of this total view
did not hesitate to enter the territory of the collective life.

In essence, their rationale was very simple. Man's final end
is to glorify God for ever in the world to come. The present life
is a preparation for such an eternal destiny, and men will both
equip themselves for it and enter it by a faithful discharge of
their immediate function in society, in the performance of
which they will be sustained by the expert ministrations which
the Church brings to them. Such helps of grace are urgently
needed, for man is a fallen creature, and if left to his own devices
and resources he will prove a prey to his own appetites, and the
final result may well be the loss of eternal blessedness. What
matters, therefore, here and now, is not that a man should grow
wealthy, should thrust himself up from one class of society to
another, exploit his neighbour and so on: but that he should so
conduct himself in this world as to prepare himself for the next.

Such facts—and to mediaeval theologians they *were* facts—
about man's existence, meant that it was the supreme responsibility of the Church, as the trustee and guardian of man's
immortal soul, to buttress up the étatism inherent in the whole
feudal structure and to fit its ethics into (or to ethicise) this framework: that is to give a divine sanction to the need for privilege
to go along with duties and for work to attract a fair reward.

Mediaeval theologians were quick to recognise how important
it was that society should not degenerate into a "free for all",
and, to prevent this, economics must never establish itself as
an autonomous science, laying down its own absolute laws,
and determining in the process what was right and wrong.

Economics was a branch of ethics, the latter dealing with the sum total of human behaviour, individual and collective. What mattered ultimately was not the stepping up of production with more goods in the shop windows: not higher and higher standards of living (indeed luxury was a dangerous snare): but a proper regard for one's own and other people's immortal souls— and this meant preserving a right balance in society.

It followed, therefore, from these basic presuppositions that the Church gave its sanction actively and passively to a rigid control of industry and agriculture, both in town and country. The craft guilds, with their apprenticeship system and monopolistic practices, were supported by ecclesiastical authority. Mediaeval theologians consequently made much of the "just price"—a price, that is, which was not determined by the fluctuations of the market, by the desperate need of the purchaser or the sheer greed of the producer; but which represented an effort to be fair and just to all concerned—to the manufacturer, the middle-man (where there was one) and the consumer. Bed-rock, of course, to this view was the contention that basic needs, and not the vagaries of the market, must determine the selling price of a commodity. Work deserves a reward, but not any reward which hard bargaining can secure. Mankind is a brotherhood, and fraternity at least demands justice. Usury was likewise forbidden (to Gentiles) because to lend on interest was to take advantage of another's necessity.

The whole endeavour of the Church was thus directed to controlling the predatory instincts of man, to preventing society becoming a jungle of competitive interests, and to do this by keeping each man in his appointed place.

The same intention is seen in the Church's concern to support and preserve the manorial system in the countryside. The strip pattern of agriculture came to be most uneconomic in that it led to bad husbandry and a great deal of wasted labour: but ecclesiastics argued that so long as it was adequate to provide basic and subsistent needs this was all that finally mattered. To encroach upon a neighbour's strip, to take advantage of his illness, or even inefficiency, to appropriate his holding would be to break up the balance of agriculture. It would invite the strong to prey on the weak. The former would thus imperil his immortal soul: the latter be plunged in desperate poverty.

It must not be thought for a single moment, however, that in practice mediaeval society was kept under such rigid control as the foregoing paragraphs suggests. Far from it. There were people who regularly broke through the control of the guilds even early in the Middle Ages, and men who added strip to strip, and thus in their small way broke up the pattern in the countryside in their anxiety to grow a little more wealthy. The merchant princes were always difficult to control. But the theological rationale of the system was more or less as I have suggested.

It can at least be said that in the Middle Ages, unlike today, there existed a sociology which was thought to grow out of Christian insights: or could be defended from within the insights of Christian theology. Economics was made to subserve ethics: and ethics were related to, and existed to promote, the ultimate "end" of mankind. That was right either in the individual or corporately in society, secular as well as religious, which enabled a man to glorify God—that is to enter through his appropriate status and particular function into (at his level) the vision of God. For this to happen, he must be protected from himself as well as from others. Thus so cautious a historian as Professor H. W. C. Davis writes: "What appeals to us in the mediaeval outlook upon life is first the idea of mankind as a brotherhood . . . secondly a profound belief in the superiority of right over might, of spirit over matter, of the eternal interests of humanity over the ambitions and the passions of the passing hours. Without Christianity these articles of faith could scarcely have passed into the common heritage of men."

The endeavour to make a social system subserve ethical ends, and the ethical ends to arise out of Christian truth, was certainly a noble one. The temptation to which the medieval theologian succumbed, however, was that, in arguing from what he believed to be the assured premises of the Faith, he converted society into a static system, without thinking it necessary to find room within it for an inner dynamic of change. Doubtless it was the influence of Roman jurisprudence which made him convert "liberty" and "justice" into legal categories. As Troeltsch comments: "The idea of a purposive and continual reform and improvement of society did not exist." The sole purpose of society was to achieve an end beyond society.

The mediaeval theologian, however, could not but be conscious (painfully at times) that man's corporate life was not as it ought to be. He could not fail to be aware of that dichotomy to which attention has so often been called—that great divide between "what is and what ought". In many respects society around him was far removed from the ideal, and at its lower levels (to quote Professor Davis again): "It was entangled in the mire and undergrowth of pathless thickets, oppressed by a still and stifling atmosphere, shut off from any view of the sky above or the pleasant plains beneath."

Men of such sincerity and candour as, for example, St. Thomas Aquinas (d. 1274) concluded that the Mediaeval Church was doing the best that it could, but in most difficult circumstances. Human nature was indeed intractable material, and the most that could be hoped for from a majority of people, particularly in the everyday ordering of society, was still very far removed from Christian living as it ought to be. Compared with the primitive bliss of the garden, man's lot was certainly impoverished: and many were the mediaeval disputations as to how extensive was the damage brought about by the Fall and whether "work" was one of its consequences.

Yet in spite of this, light was shining steadily through the surrounding darkness. One set of men (and women), so the mediaeval theologians believed, bore witness to Christian virtue in a purer and less adulterated form. These were the holy men, living in communities, who devoted themselves entirely to the religious and corporate life, and were themselves vowed to poverty, chastity, and obedience. In a polluted world, these monasteries constituted little cells where the fruits of the Kingdom, "love, joy, and peace in believing", could be realised, in as nearly perfect a form as was possible for imperfect men.

So did mediaeval piety commit itself to the conception of a double standard (though not in the same person)—the standard capable of achievement in the more rarefied atmosphere of the monastery, and the standard which, though falling short of this, was yet adequate in the world outside.

This conception presents difficulties to the modern mind, and lays itself open to many objections. The double standard, it must be noticed, does not result from different levels of the will to goodness, but from the nature of the environment in which men live and in which the will operates. This view accepts that the life of the world, with its coercive jurisdiction and necessary chores, is peculiarly resistant to the ethics of the Kingdom, but that most people must live within it.

Many Christians would dispute the premises on which this whole reasoning is based, and indeed would regard the conclusions as almost pernicious. The distinction, they would argue, is either unreal or improper. To regard one kind of vocation as higher than another is to weaken the whole conception of vocation and the reality of the Incarnation. This may be true, and it must be allowed that into the exaltation of the celibate life as in its nature higher, a great deal of false asceticism (and the influence of dualistic philosophies) have entered in. A second best is never adequate, for man is called to his highest possible attainment.

Yet the reasons for making the distinction remain important, and it may be claimed, I think, that behind the thesis of the double standard there is at least a frankness, and the recognition of a problem, which no subsequent thinkers have been able effectively to dispose of. Mediaeval theologians were honestly anxious to be practical, but not to lower ultimate standards in the process. They recognised, with Aristotle, that men must be taken as they are, if they are to be made into what they ought to be. They believed, further, that when higher motives proved ineffective lower ones must be brought into play: and that coercion, though regrettable, had to be used to keep erring man from wandering too far from the straight and narrow way. But they were candid enough to admit that such ought not to be: it was due to the weakness of men, and to the accumulative effect upon society of man's sin. Society as at present organised fell far short of the Kingdom of God.

These theologians certainly did not pull wool over their own eyes. There *was* a distinctive Christian virtue which the world, even when organised within a Christian framework, did not display. The Kingdom was indeed social in its nature, and if its only embodiment was the sinful and consequently ambiguous world around, no clear beacon of light would be shining in the half darkness. Faced with what they regarded as this grim prospect, mediaeval theologians accepted realistically that a diffused society, preoccupied with the means of living, did not seem capable, even at its highest levels, of being lifted into the full light of the Kingdom of God, though individuals here and there (the Saints) might, through the grace of God, distinguish themselves by remarkable holiness. It was society as a whole, however, in its corporate manifestation, that the theologians were equally concerned about. God, in His infinite mercy, accepted the imperfect offering of the world—but, equally in His mercy, called some men to a separated, though community life, so that there, the Kingdom (yet even there not absolutely, for that is impossible in this passing world) might be established. There were blemishes even in the monasteries—these were the spots that defiled the robe—but the intention of the rule was perfection. In the world, not even its highest ambitions (corporately) could be made expressive of the Kingdom.

If there is a degree of confused thinking in such a point of view, it yet honestly faces up to a real difficulty, going back to the early days of the Church, and arising out of the distinctive virtue of Jesus. The thesis of the double standard has the merit of being prepared to admit that there is something distinctive in Christian witness and absolute in the demands which it makes: it refuses to equate a fully integrated Christian discipleship with that which is often mistaken for it; and it accepts frankly that there is a tension between the ideal and the actual, with the result that for most men even their best endeavours, and the collective witness of society, fall short of the glory of God. Man remains an unprofitable servant.

But the unprofitable servant is still a servant, so that even though the perfect witness is relegated to the monasteries yet a Christian witness is possible (and is required) in the world, though the nature of such a witness must be adjusted and accommodated to the situation of fallen men.

These mediaeval theologians had little respect for an ethic which could in no way be realised in the ordinary day to day life of men and nations. Thus from many a pulpit, and in simple catechisms, teaching was given about work; about the conduct of trade; about the relations of one class to another; about the responsibility of privilege, and the respect due to "degree"— and so on. And what was said in this context was believed to safeguard man's final end, and therefore by implication his present welfare. But lest the common man should presume, he was pointed to the religious communities where dedicated and sacrificial men bore witness to the ultimate standards of God's Kingdom.

CHAPTER VII

THE BIRTH OF THE MODERN WORLD

"THE MIDDLE AGES" is a descriptive term used only for our convenience. "They" never existed in pure form, for the process of disintegration, here a little there a little, set in even before they reached their peak of achievement. In the fifteenth and sixteenth centuries, it is now clear that one phase of civilisation was giving place to another. Once again (as at the break-up of the Roman Empire) collapse went along with great political and economic changes. The emergence of the spirit of nationalism; the concentration of effective power in the hands of the "Prince"; the birth of a bold experimentalism, inspired in part by the rediscovery of the humanistic and non-Christian culture of Greece (which, as a civilisation, seemed to have done quite well); the voyages of discovery and the opening up of new trade routes; the advent of a new psychology which saw the universe as something to investigate, to enjoy, and to exploit— all these eventually brought to an end the old restricted, local and controlled economy of the Middle Ages. Merchant princes had for long found that if they cut through the control exercised by the guilds they could add considerably to their financial reward. Lords of the manor equally discovered that if only they could get rid of the traditional yet ridiculous strips, they could then proceed to lay down their estates to pasture, and thereby enormously increase their income.

Thus it was that strong financial incentives operated to break up the old customary economy both in town and country. After all, so it was (perhaps unconsciously) argued, why should some men not grow wealthy? It was all very well to deny oneself satisfactions in order to reap blessedness in the life to come: but why not begin by making the best of the present? At least, here was a tangible reality, and it would be a pity to turn one's back on it in anticipation of a future reward. Wasn't it possible to have both? And didn't the Christian Faith itself invite men to look in both directions? Surely there was nothing wrong in a man expressing himself economically, artistically and nationally? And ought not ethical behaviour to be seen in this much larger context? Wasn't there a need for a more activist, more positive, indeed a more ruthless morality capable of inspiring the new assertion of man?

To this contemporary mood the individualism implicit in the whole movement of the Reformation contributed, sometimes in spite of its leaders, who were on the whole "ethically conservative". Renaissance man felt that he had the ball at his feet, and he decided that he must give it a kick, even though its course might be a little unpredictable and get in other people's way. A new attitude was being born, and it was not easy to see at a first glance how the ethics of the Kingdom, as mediaeval man had come to understand them, fitted into it.

The question could not finally be avoided as to how Christian teaching was related to this expansionist economy, and more generally to this new assertion of man. That the new economy did step up production no objective observer could doubt, though the increased wealth was distributed into few hands and left poverty in its wake.

In this situation, what could the Christian preacher and moralist say? The simple, though regrettable, fact is that in the sixteenth century, and later, most of them just did not know what to say—except to deplore present developments and to urge the reinstatement of the traditional economy. Bishop Latimer in his famous sermon on "The Plough" deplores the depopulation of the countryside and sees it as due to wicked men anxious only to grow rich; but he offers no solution (perhaps it was not his responsibility to do so) other than to look back nostalgically to the past. Basically, this was the view of Archbishop Laud in the seventeenth century. The inability of Christian leaders to offer a positive critique, accepting but trying to direct the new energies, was a tragedy for which posthumous sackcloth and ashes can hardly atone. At a time when new forces were being unleashed, forces in part called forth by the inherent dynamic, the stress on particularity, and the general thought forms of Christian Faith, it was essential that that Faith should live in the present and react positively to the contemporary challenge. Prophecy which springs as much from ignorance as moral indignation is not likely to prove very effective. Perhaps the ecclesiastical founders of the Royal Society were wiser.

So far as there was religious teaching which tried to say anything concerning the social and economic scene in the early days (this was not so true of the political) it was simply regretful of the past, and later merely consecrated what came to exist. Unable to handle the problems which arose economically out of the collective life, churchmen retreated from this sphere into an arid individualism. The Ten Commandments were preached up: the class structure and the rights of property were regarded as sacrosanct: and the individual citizen was assured that he would do his duty best by fitting himself into this overall pattern. To keep sacred the marriage bond: not to steal; not to covet (this was most important!); to worship God on Sundays—these and other injunctions like them were the whole duty of man.

The result was that both the slave trade and the industrial revolution pursued their way without an informed Christian critique. When in 1776 Adam Smith produced, in his "Wealth of Nations", what was considered a scientific rationale for the new economics, his essential thesis was accepted as almost equally authoritative in its own sphere as Newton's "In Principio" in another. In brief this respectable Scottish Professor of Moral Philosophy maintained that economics was a science, almost in the same way that physics was a science—and the other inductive disciplines. If men were left free to pursue their own economic advantage (which is precisely what they would do if left free) they would buy in the cheapest and sell in the dearest market. By such activity they would promote the general well-being of the nation; since ruthless competition leads to efficiency, increases production, and consequently lowers costs.

Thus it is that by a merciful dispensation of Providence ("an invisible hand") what might seem universal selfishness is made to subserve a universal good. Of course some people, in this struggle, will go to the wall—they can be, morally must be, assisted by private charity—but on no account should the delicately adjusted economic mechanism be tampered with. The state (government) should keep out of it, except, perhaps, now and again to insert a little oil into the works. To interfere with it over much would be as rational as to try, by legislation, to alter the laws of physics.

Indeed, so Adam Smith seems to assume, economics *is* an autonomous science, and it cannot be made, in itself, subordinate to alien moral principles. It constitutes its own norms, and must not be regarded as a branch of traditional ethics, the latter being based on quite different criteria. General ethical principles cannot be directly applied to it.

The above may seem somewhat of a caricature, but I believe that it substantially states the logical implications of the position which Adam Smith took up. Its merits, though some may be dangerous half truths, should not, however, be forgotten. There is a sense in which abstract ethical judgements cannot be applied, from outside, to different human disciplines. To introduce ethical criteria into man's economic activities means knowing something about economics, and knowing this from within. The mistake of

Adam Smith was to isolate man's economic appetites from other and equally compelling drives to action. Pure and unmixed motives seldom exist.

The problem for sincere Christians, themselves the children of their own day and generation, was not easy, and it is unfair to be too critical of their bemusement. Nor was the kind of apologia for the new mercantilism, outlined above, confined only to economics. Machiavelli's "Prince", written over two centuries earlier, had suggested that the state, as embodied in the person of the ruler, was equally freed from traditional moral restraints, and could manufacture its own code of behaviour. The fact is that Machiavelli, imbued with the spirit of a rising nationalism and disgusted with the anarchy of his day, wanted a strong government, and was prepared to subordinate almost everything else to the paramount need for law and order. The Prince, therefore, might do almost anything so long as he regarded it as serving the supposed interests of his nation. Thomas Hobbes in his "Leviathan" (1651) took largely the same position, committing himself to an atomistic view of society and regarding every nation as being in respect of every other nation in a condition, if not of war, at least of lawlessness.

The new omni-competent state, with supreme authority vested in the monarch (later in England in the King in Parliament), certainly constituted a grave problem for post-renaissance theologians, comparable in the political sphere to that which obtained in the social and economic. True the Coronation Service used in England recognised that there were sanctities which the monarch dare not invade: and that finally it was not force which constituted right but conformity to God's will: but at the purely practical level there was no power which could call the sovereign state to account.

Such moral absolutism had subtle and therefore not easily observable repercussions upon behaviour patterns between societies. At least Medieval Christendom, in spite of fratricidal wars and a great deal of local anarchy, did subscribe to the principle of an international order; and Sir Thomas More went to his death as a witness to this wider loyalty. Grotius (1583-1645) tried to revive it.

The fervent nationalisms of the post renaissance world, developing a mystique and a will to power as they went along, have certainly proved shatteringly destructive in the life of Europe, and it is unfortunately true to say that they have never been brought within an effective Christian direction. Some Christians indeed have been so far misled as to confuse loyalty to their own nation as loyalty to the Kingdom—it may of course, in certain circumstances, form part of it—and to convert every enemy into a barbarian at the gate. Anti-Christian has been given a wide and generous interpretation, varying as occasion demanded from Catholic Louis to the Mohammedan Mahdi. Perhaps Hegel, with the best intention, has had something to do with this near deification of the nation: and the failure of Christian theologians to provide a satisfactory philosophy of the state, arising organically out of their own body of truth, has not made the situation any more easy. Even such a sensitive theologian as F. D. Maurice, during the expansionist phase of Victorian England, saw great religious significance in, and even became enthusiastic over, the Crimean War.

The tragedy is that a new world struggling for expression, anxious to assert the particularity of men and nations, found the social philosophy it inherited from the Middle Ages static and naïvely moralistic when it came to practical questions. In the sphere of politics it was equally legalistic, finding no elbow room for dynamic change.

But to return to the new mercantilism of "laissez-faire, laissez-passer", it seemed to be quite impossible, until well on in the nineteenth century, for a Christian theology to embark upon an informed criticism of the ethical attitude it presupposed. The reason for this is all too apparent. It felt unable to do so without questioning the basic presuppositions on which "laissez-faire" rested, and these were thought to be established almost beyond argument. The bankruptcy of eighteenth-century theologians when it came to Christian sociological teaching—in spite of Butler's great work in the more strictly moral sphere—is pathetic. Many of them were certainly anxious to soften the harshness of much contemporary living, and to do their duty to their less fortunate brethren: but they were too wedded to a static conception of society which they had inherited (and which they thought to be Christian) to be able to apply their theology to the new economics. They did not feel free, therefore to criticise the system. Society was too delicate a mechanism, and they dare not tamper with it, except occasionally to apply a little grease to the parts. They dare not jump up into the driving cabin.

When Edmund Burke moved away from mechanism to organism, it was still felt that a certain amount of disease was inevitable, and that to operate would cause the death of the patient—or what was even worse, revolution as in France. The practical result was the preaching up of private charity, and liberally did many a simple Christian respond, as the walls of countless church towers bear eloquent, if somewhat dusty, witness. Dr. Thomas Sherlock, Bishop of London, merely reiterated what was commonly accepted when he asserted that the poor have a right to work (for the rich)—or if unable to do this, through unemployment, age, or infirmity, to charity. The rich correspondingly had a duty to provide either work or relief. Such teaching was regarded as economically sound and yet within its limits Christian. William Wilberforce added an additional comfort by congratulating the poor on being mercifully (and providentially) delivered both from the responsibilities and temptations which wealth brings—an echo of mediaevalism without, perhaps, the same degree of insight.

It is easy, I repeat, to sit in judgement on these misguided theologians who retreated so completely from the economic field. They felt themselves, however, to be amateurs in a highly expert and technical department of knowledge. A distinctive Christian witness must find its outlet in personal integrity in home and family, in the virtues of thrift and hard work, and by the rich in charity: but charity could not be introduced into the iron law of wages which were determined by other and more economic criteria.

It is always easy to be wise after the event: though one cannot but wish that eighteenth-century theologians had not been stampeded or overawed into allowing Christian insights to be thus ousted from the social and economic fields. The study of moral theology was in fact almost abandoned in any creative or original way. To be always a little suspicious of experts constitutes a healthy state of mind: and anyhow there ought to have been a field, if these theologians had but cultivated it, in which they themselves were experts. The cry to keep either religion or ethics out of politics and economics is like asking to keep coal out of an engine or the Archbishop of Canterbury out of Lambeth Palace.

The clue to an understanding of this retreat is to be found in what was happening in the day to day world.

The eighteenth and nineteenth centuries were a period when the area of assured scientific results was rapidly growing larger, and when inductive methods applied to the physical sciences were beginning to yield enormous practical results. The temper of mind to which this success gave birth made it seem difficult (even illegitimate) for theologians to introduce into the ordering of the common life traditional moral categories. The apparent ruthlessness of "natural selection", of the evolutionary process as a whole, if it engendered an ultimate optimism, yet seemed to adjust men's minds to struggle, pain and warfare, and thus to make distinctive Christians virtues at least a little premature—though Huxley was prepared to affirm that man should be moral against the universe.

To talk of "love", except within a very limited terrain, against the background of a process in which value emerged only painfully out of disvalue, and as a result of ruthless strife, untold waste, and great suffering, seemed to bespeak much sentiment in the heart but not excessive intelligence in the head. Were not the qualities (virtues) necessary to be victorious in the struggle (i.e. to survive and by surviving to allow the higher to triumph over the lower)—were not these of necessity the virtues which the Absolute (if unconscious) Will behind all things was working to elicit? For the weak to go to the wall, for the strong to inherit the earth seemed to be part of the plan. The shade of Nietzsche and his "slave morality" are beginning to appear over the horizon.

The first serious attack theologically in England on the economic theories of Adam Smith was that adumbrated by F. D. Maurice, who, after being deprived of a chair at King's College, London, finally ended his days as Professor of Moral Philosophy at Cambridge. Maurice felt in his bones that an economic theory which proved so vicious that the government had been forced to ignore it in its Factory Legislation, just could not be "true" even in this sinful world—that is if in any real sense it is God's world. Yet Maurice was anxious not to put himself in a position where he could easily be ruled out of court by the facile criticism that his heart had triumphed over his head. Though he was himself violently opposed to systems and always suspicious of them, what he wanted, and what he sought, was a living principle, arising out of an assured premise which he could use to rebut (what he regarded as) an immoral and pernicious economic practice.

It will seem surprising to some that he found this principle in what is often regarded as the most academic, remote and philosophic of all Christian doctrines.

Maurice began by asking himself in the light of Christian Faith and Christian experience what was the basic structure of the spiritual ground behind existence. He found the answer in the doctrine of the Trinity, that glimpse into the Being of God which shows Him as living an intense "family" or personal life. In God there is difference and yet unity, a coming together in love, without confusion of persons. Here is the final expression of fulfilled living, and therefore the pattern to which all creative human relationships must conform.

From this premise, it was not difficult for Maurice, given his theological point of view, to go on to maintain that the so-called "iron laws of economics" were no laws at all. They were bogus and invalid because they were opposed, in their very nature, to the structure of final reality as it exists in God. They were an abstraction and did not correspond with the facts; for it will be found that every worth-while economic enterprise is successful only in so far as men work with one another in a common cause. To regard every man's hand as against every other man's hand, and to erect an economic system on this basis, just will not do. The industrial life of a nation cannot be treated in this inhuman way.

There is no need to comment on the soundness or otherwise of Maurice's sociological conclusions: what is important is to notice his endeavour to found a sociology on specifically Christian affirmations. It is typical of his whole approach to social morality (this is his own term) that he entered the field as a theologian, and regarded this, not as a disqualification, but as his one claim to speak. Theology to Maurice is the foundation science, and as such should be capable of directing other disciplines: it is the ground upon which they all rest, and is uniquely aware of their mutual relations. Thus Maurice is prepared to condemn an economic thesis because it violates an insight which is central to Christian Faith.

That Maurice, in spite of the obscurity of his style, is being rediscovered in this day and generation suggests that many feel the need of a more consistent and distinctive approach to contemporary problems. In saying this, it also needs to be said that Christianity to Maurice is no propositional religion and he may well be regarded as in some respects an existentialist before his time.

It must be admitted, of course, that the social problem is not quite so unambiguous as F. D. Maurice supposed it, which is probably only to say that he was a prophet and lived at a time when some public issues were more sharply defined. Where he blazed a trail, others such as Westcott, Gore and Temple have followed. The Christian today, however, no longer shares Maurice's confidence as to the possibility of directly relating the insights of his Faith to the moral problems arising within a collective technological society. His real difficulty lies in the novelty of the situation: and the ambiguities of his own insights.

On many major questions relating to contemporary society, Christian opinion is hopelessly divided, and where it is unanimous, its conclusions do not seem necessarily to arise organically out of the Faith. The impact of the late Dr. William Temple on public opinion is interesting in this respect. The undoubted appeal which he made to the man in the street lay in the fact that he was obviously concerned to relate Christian truth to everyday life, and to introduce into economics more personal categories. His public speeches, and his little book in the Penguin series, "Christianity and the Social Order", bear obvious testimony to this life-long concern, though this does not necessarily mean that his economic teaching was always very well informed. It was what he stood for, rather than what he

D

precisely said, which became significant for most people, who snatched eagerly at an exposition of economics which stressed justice and even sympathy.

So far as the contemporary world is concerned, whether it is the profit motive, the hydrogen bomb, race relationships, birth control, homosexuality, A.I.D., divorce, the reunion of Christendom—the list could be almost endlessly prolonged—there is no one Christian view, because there is no common agreement as to how the ethics of the Kingdom are related to particular situations in the world. The result is that a great deal of so-called Christian opinion on morals and politics in fact consists simply of speculations which have no necessary relation with revealed Christian truth, and are consequently of such a nature that any mature person of reasonable good will might hold them. This does not for a moment invalidate such opinions: it only means they are not distinctively Christian.

This comment may well serve as a jumping off ground for the discussion in our next chapter.

IV: MAINLY THEOLOGICAL

CHAPTER VIII

REALISM AND COMMITMENT

IN THE PRECEDING chapter reference was made to the mediaeval thesis of the double standard, which was an attempt to do justice to the actual without losing sight of the ideal. As such it endeavoured to face up to the almost inevitable tension between absolute standards seen in Jesus which must obtain in his Kingdom, and the poverty of achievement which many devout Christians feel to be the best that can be hoped for in a sinful world.

It is now necessary to examine in somewhat more detail this effort after realism, which may perhaps be done the more vividly if we use again, as an illustration (and for the purpose of illustration only), the Christian attitude to war. It is always more profitable, when Christian ethics are under discussion, to be as concrete and particular as possible.

The early orthodoxy of pacifism gave way, gradually at first but more rapidly in the reign of Constantine, under the pressure of a new historic situation, until at the end of the fourth century this particular witness had almost entirely ceased to exist. Yet theologians in the Middle Ages could not be indifferent to the dilemma which war poses, or ought to pose, to the devout and dedicated Christian, and they consequently set about to answer the question how such a man (and society) could conscientiously take part in it. The result was what is usually called the thesis of "The Just War", which may be briefly stated as follows.

War is, and must always remain, an evil, since it unleashes violence; and for its successful prosecution demands virtues, and employs techniques, far removed from the ethics of the Kingdom which are love, joy and peace. It would be unthinkable to regard war, in any situation, as in conformity with God's perfect will for mankind. In heaven the sword must give place to the ploughshare. But the world is a sinful, fallen world, corrupted by man's rebellion against God, and though it is obviously "wrong" to resort to war, it may, in certain circumstances, be even more "wrong" not to resort to it—that is, the sum total of evil resulting from not prosecuting the war may be greater than from prosecuting it. There are extreme crises in the affairs of creaturely man when, within certain carefully defined limits, it is permissible for a Christian to "serve in the wars". Such a war is just if the following criteria are respected:

1) It must be fought in a just cause—i.e. it must be non-aggressive, etc.

2) The intention in fighting the war must also be just.

3) Every other means (e.g. arbitration, conciliation) must have been tried and proved ineffective. War is a last and desperate resort like a surgical operation.

4) The state of warfare must be declared by a properly constituted authority. War must never be complete lawlessness.

5) The means used in fighting the war must be just. War can never be regarded as total or absolute. It must be contained within some overall pattern, otherwise victory would be completely sterile.

6) The competent authority which embarks upon war must be reasonably certain of victory, or at least of securing the end for which it is being fought. This apparently non-heroic requirement is important. Since war is in itself an evil and remains so, there can be no value in fighting as such. To use violence in this way only becomes morally tolerable when it is likely to prove effective in establishing or preserving a measure of justice.

7) It must be reasonably inferred that the evils resulting from fighting will be less than the evils resulting from not fighting.

Such conditions invite the obvious comment that they are highly theoretical and certainly non-realistic to a degree. They are as such quite incapable of being applied in practice. Who is to determine what is an aggressive war? Is a preventive war, for example, aggressive? Who can judge "intention"? Can anybody of men ever assess the possible consequences of waging and not waging war? And anyhow what yard-stick or value-judgement can be applied in making this assessment, since justice is a very ambiguous concept, and self-deception is all too easy. Is it not true that in practice every nation convinces itself, and without much difficulty, of the rectitude of its own cause? Anyhow, is the individual free to make his own judgement in such matters?

These criticisms can hardly be refuted. Political judgements are seldom made in an atmosphere of calm detachment such as would make this kind of debate feasible. This was the case even in the more leisurely days of the Middle Ages.

Contemporary theologians, of course, were perfectly aware of these difficulties. Yet such criticisms do not entirely take away from the significance, and in some respects the value, of the presuppositions which lie behind the statement of the just war. The argument was meant to establish a climate of thought, to engender over the years a way of looking at things, to inculcate a pattern of thinking.

Essentially this thesis represents a frank recognition, by theologians, of the dangers inherent in the exercise of power, and the desperate need to control and restrain its use. Governments are in the nature of the case equipped with a coercive jurisdiction: and it must therefore be the concern of the Christian that this power does not get out of hand, nor become absolutely destructive. Somehow or other, and no matter how non-ideal the contrivance may seem to be, power must be employed to offset power, when justice is menaced and in the balance.

Yet involved in this concern to deal with the abuse of power, there went also a frank recognition of the limits of "offsetting" power. There are many ends which violence of itself cannot realise: and there may be some evils which are better endured than remedied by a resort to force, of which the outcome cannot be foreseen. Warfare can never be more than just tolerable. It represents a lower standard, and in this respect the theologians were wiser than the ballad makers, though the exponents of romantic chivalry were themselves also concerned to consecrate power.

The thesis of the just war also represents, in those who expounded it, a determination not to let history get out of hand, and to control the relations between states so that the strong do not prey on the weak. Behind it there lay some conception of an international order: of the protection of rights and (in the feudal sense of the word) liberties. Such a view is clearly opposed to the self-authenticating state-absolutism of Machiavelli, since it recognises that justice is something other than the uneasy result of an equilibrium of force, or that which a crude will to power is able to dictate. That which is just (as the just price), in idea at least, is that which recognises the legitimate claims of all parties concerned, and which ought to obtain if an impartial judgement were possible. Of course justice so conceived can hardly be realised in fact, and it was inevitable that it should be thought of in static and not in dynamic terms. Still such justice is better, as an ideal, than no justice at all.

From this summary statement, it is obvious that the thinking lying behind the concept of the just war tries to face up to the implications of an ambiguous situation. Its presupposition is that Christians cannot contract out of the world—i.e. that God encounters a man in his function as citizen—or be indifferent to the strife of conflicting groups, though this may mean dirtying his hands. The ethics of the Kingdom cannot always be directly introduced into the political and social life, though Christians are still challenged by God to accept responsibility for the ordering of everyday affairs, and to do the best they can. If coercive power can never be used to beget love, this does not mean that it cannot be deployed to maintain an external justice—imperfect though such a distributive justice may be.

It is understandable that the view above stated, though in not so refined a way, should have been used across the centuries to justify a Christian participation in war. Doubtless such thinking (non-articulate, maybe) persuaded many Christians in England and elsewhere to feel it right to fight against Germany both in 1914 and 1939. It cannot, however, be used to justify an all out nuclear war.

Yet one question, and an important question, remains to be asked. Has this thesis of the just war any organic relation to Christian Faith? By this I mean, does it arise out of any specifically Christian insights? Or is it a view which can be held by deduction from such general premises as have no necessary connection with specifically Christian truth?

The immediate answer would seem to be that it is possible for any well-disposed person, though he does not believe the Christian Faith to be true, to accept this thesis in its most general application, and consequently to base his conduct upon it. Indeed many do. This does not, in itself, imply for a moment that Christians ought not to commit themselves to it: only that they do not necessarily owe anything to their Faith when they do so, and that no particular Christian insight is involved. Nor, it may be supposed, did mediaeval theologians, who asserted that the unassisted reason could establish the existence of God and the objectivity of the moral law, claim that it did. All that the exponents of the just war thesis need assume is that certain social and political situations are better (that is more just) than others, and that, in trying to secure the former, resort to violence is sometimes a regrettable necessity—maybe even a grim duty.

Some Christians, however would maintain that Christian Faith gives to justice a greater claim to respect, as representing, in a given situation, the will of God: and that although such justice falls short of what ought to obtain in God's Kingdom, yet it is nearer to it than a state of injustice. The fruits of the Kingdom may the more easily grow in a society in which there is already an elementary pattern of justice, than in one in which it finds no place. Thus, the value judgement made, in respect of the factual consequences flowing from making, or declining, a particular act of war, owes a great deal to a Christian insight.

It is at this point, perhaps, that we can best consider an ethical position which attempts to give some kind of theological sanction to the thinking which lies behind the thesis of the just war—an ethical position, it may be observed in passing, to which Dr. Reinhold Niebuhr and Archbishop William Temple, to mention only two, have subscribed. I shall call it the "realist position" for convenience and recognition.

The realistic view begins by seeing man as essentially a fallen creature, who, since he lives both in nature and supernature, bedevils himself and infects his environment by his constant rebellion against God. If the Christian, within this kind of world, is in any sense (particularly in the collective life) to promote effectively the purposes of God, he must realistically recognise this situation for what it is. As a practical guide, therefore, he must ask what course of action is likely to have the most desirable consequences—that is promote rather than hinder the Kingdom. Maybe the choice before him is not often (though occasionally it will be) between two lines of action one of which is absolutely good and the other absolutely evil in respect of its supposed consequences. More often he is caught up in the ambiguities of the human predicament and is himself moved to action by a variety of motives. Sometimes whatever he does—and he must do something—is in a measure evil in its consequences. Thus in making his choice he is often confronted by a situation in which all he can hope to do is to decide for the lesser of two evils: and there are occasions when he feels an obligation to discharge duties which are mutually exclusive—if he does the one he cannot do the other, as so often happens with a woman caught up in the conflicting loyalties to her parents and her own family. Whatever the solution, she will be left with the nagging feeling that she has neglected, or, at least not discharged a duty.

If such constitutes man's real existential situation, any attempt to realise a perfectionist Christian ethic can be self-stultifying, almost a selfish indulgence in a private pietism, as if it is better to feel good than to do good. Such conduct ends by being irreparably escapist rather than challenging to effective action. Such perfectionism means that the Christian ceases to be really effective, because he removes himself so far from the real world which sinful men inhabit that he has no influence upon it. By declining, often, to handle power, he does nothing to restrain its wrongful deployment.

To put this argument in an extreme form, to seek to indulge in a perfectionist (or supposedly perfectionist) ethic in a sinful world is to fall into the insidious temptation of a subtle spiritual pride, which serves to keep a man's hands clean when they *ought* to be dirty. Also it has the paradoxical effect of imposing upon others, whom the Christian ought (humbly) to think of as not so well equipped as himself, the responsibility of exercising authority in situations where evil is most rampant. In un-regenerate hands, may it not be that the measure of compromise, inevitable in a sinful world, becomes greater than it need be, and the adjustment is made at far too low a level?

The late Dr. William Temple gave the following excellent illustration of the realist approach to Christian commitment in a sinful world. Let us suppose that a dedicated Christian owns a business in a branch of industry where competition is cut-throat and the standard of commercial integrity not very high. If he sets out to realise a near perfectionist ethic (standard) his business will probably go bankrupt, the shareholders will certainly be up in arms, his employees and himself out of a job. As a result, this particular branch of industry will be the poorer for ceasing to have working within it a man who might have done something to raise its general level. Is not his real, if more difficult, task to carry on in the business, and progressively lift up common practice, so long as he can keep his own concern going? Doubtless if he does this, the temptation will be to conduct it at a level lower than the highest practically possible, but, dei gratia, he can resist this. In accepting this necessary compromise, the Christian businessman (says Dr. Temple) is right to encourage himself with the thought that in his given situation this compromise is God's will. Of course, there may come a time when he begins to feel that the standard necessary to keep in the business is so low that no possible Christian witness can be made within it, and that he would be more effective by walking out. But such a judgement can only be made by himself and within the total situation.

No one can deny the deep sincerity of those who hold this view, nor the appeal which it makes to prudence and common sense: but the criticisms which have been brought to bear upon it are of importance in any general discussion of Christian ethics. True such criticisms, in so far as they set up an alternative system, hardly come to grips with the realist theory on its own ground. The battle is rather like that which would ensue if an elephant declared war upon a whale. Both views may seem to be right in their own field and given their different starting points. This is why so often, in discussion of seemingly opposed ethical views, one is left with the feeling that both are right within their own terms of reference—a conclusion which is not always a happy one, when it comes to deciding practical questions, and ethics is a most practical affair.

It has been asserted, as a criticism of the realist view, that it is all very well to dilate as to conflicts of loyalty, to assert that even in our best intentions we remain unprofitable servants: but may not this in practice, so far as the ordinary believer is concerned, tend to blunt the edge of moral endeavour? Has not the follower of Jesus the right to a good conscience when in given circumstances he has honestly tried to do his best? Surely to be encouraged by such a satisfaction is not to indulge in spiritual pride, nor to parade one's virtue, but simply to experience the support which a fond parent gives to a struggling child. Essential to ethical success (if such a phrase may be employed) is the assurance that when we have, with integrity, and seeking such guidance as we can, committed ourselves to a line of action, we can do so whole-heartedly, without the doubt that saps the mind. As Sir Francis Drake's prayer has it:

"O Lord God, when thou givest to thy servants to endeavour any great matter, grant us to know that it is not the beginning but the continuing of the same until it be thoroughly finished, which yieldeth the true glory; through him that for the finishing of thy work laid down his life, Our Redeemer, Jesus Christ."

Any inhibition that weakens the will, which breaks down a reasonable confidence, or causes mental reservations, will impair the effectiveness of action. It has been well said: "He who hesitates, his chance is lost." The man who keeps on asking whether he has married the right wife is not likely to make a happy marriage.

It may be replied to this criticism that the man who embarks upon the lesser of two evils *can* do so with a thoroughly good conscience; because in his situation, this is the "right" thing for him to do, i.e. God's will for him. But the criticism outlined above is not so much concerned with a theoretical justification as with the psychological effects, over a period of years, upon the ordinary person who accepts and is conditioned by this point of view.

The realist position is further open to criticism just where it seems to be most sure of itself—that is in its claim to deal with men as they are rather than, in our more Utopian moments, we would wish them to be. May not this very realism, by reminding men constantly of the ambiguity of their position, make it more ambiguous than it need be? In refusing to countenance any form of perfectionism, does it not *in practice* subtly encourage a man to fall below even the level of his possible attainment, particularly since it insists that human nature is very weak and sinful. For this reason it has been maintained that the real weakness of this ethical position is that it all too easily persuades a man to "opt" for the second best, and gives him apparent justification for so doing. True a man in thinking himself so justified has misunderstood the nature of this ethical position, but the practical danger is that he may easily misunderstand it. Without appearing too Machiavellian (or Irish!) it might cynically be claimed that even if the realist view were true in this respect, it would be better for the ordinary man not to know it—and this for an obvious reason.

The temptation for most fallible Christians is not to try to live up to an absolute ethic, and to be discouraged by finding this impossible: but to live at a much lower level than they could in fact achieve. To feel the full weight of the challenge "Be ye perfect as your Father in Heaven is perfect," may well prove more invigorating to the will and more encouraging finally to goodness. A feeble conscience often grows more feeble the more it is tended.

A third, and far more serious objection to the realist view, is that this ethical position rests upon a double psychical act—a judgement of fact as to probable consequences flowing from a particular course of action, and a judgement of value in respect of those consequences. To quote Dr. Temple's words: "In (applying the standards of his religion) the Christian is bound to consider the probable effects of any course of action and choose that which in its consequences is likely to promote the greatest conformity to those standards."

No one can deny that a calculation of consequences plays some part in ethical judgements in particular situations, but is it always decisive, or ought it to be, when a man comes to act? Might it not be claimed that in his most significant and critical moral judgements a man experiences a strong sense of compulsion, and that this experience of constraint is as if he must do this particular deed even though the heavens fall—though of course, some (it may be almost unconscious) awareness of possible consequences, due to an accumulated experience over the years, may well enter into this total moral response? When, for example, Latimer said to Ridley at the stake: "Play the man Ridley and we shall light such a candle as shall never be put out", he was not making an immediate estimate of the probable results flowing from their martyrdom. Rather this conviction sprang from a prior act of faith in God, and a belief in His Providence.

Perhaps it may be said that Jesus on the Cross was not preoccupied with consequences as such—that was God's affair: his own concern was to be true to a particular commitment.

The critique just stated now needs to be taken a little further. Not only do people not, as a matter of fact, calculate consequences in their most critical moral judgements, but if they attempt to do so it is doubtful what dependability such calculations can have. Dr. H. H. Farmer says of this exercise that it is "merely the natural reason calculating probabilities upon data drawn from the past mainly unregenerate experiences of the race."

Certainly such an estimate of possible consequences can only be attempted with any confidence on the assumption that we are dealing with a fairly closed system, in which the future will be as the past. Biblical history hardly bears out this assumption. God must be either ruled out of account, or He must be brought into the system, for no one can hope to estimate the results of His Providential activity, as if it were merely one ingredient amongst others. Particularly difficult, it would seem, is it to make this calculation and compare it with what would happen if different commitments had been undertaken.

In reply to this kind of criticism, it has been contended that the realist view does justice to "constraint" and "commitment" by supposing that man experiences a general sense of compulsion to do whatever he believes to be right. What the rational judgement does in estimating probable consequences is merely to canalise the moral drive in a particular behaviour pattern.

But is such a distinction capable of being maintained? And is it true to the deepest Christian experience? I think not, for the religious man in the divine-human encounter is not informed with a general moral enlightenment, from which right action results by a process of deduction; but rather he "hears" a call to particular action. Thus Abram is made aware of a voice, uttering a positive command: "Get thee out of thy country, and from thy kindred, and from thy father's house unto a land that I will show thee": and Isaiah experiences a particular challenge: "Whom shall I send, and who will go for us?"

Form and content are here merged into one, in an experience of absolute demand which goes along with what has been described as "final succour". God deals with His children as persons, in the positions where they existentially are, and in the context of their particular commitments and life history.

Are these two views, the one which places the emphasis on a calculation of consequences, and the other which stresses constraint and commitment, incompatible? As has been hinted earlier, the distinction is obviously not absolute. There is an element of commitment in the first, and unconscious habitual calculation (if such a use of terms is permissible) in the second. Yet this does not mean that the distinction is unreal: rather, I think, that the one or the other is more prominent according to the kind of decision that a man is called upon to make: or the kind of person who makes it.

In most of the moral decisions in everyday life, the probable results of our action largely help to determine the choice that we make—and a great deal of life is lived at this ordinary, perhaps unexciting, level. If a man asked a revolver of us (this is a little more exciting) we should probably not give it to him because of the uses to which he might put it.

On the other hand, in the great crises of life, where there is a deep and almost agonising personal concern, and a man is "poured out like water", he may come through it to experience constraint and obligation. What matters to him then more than anything else is faithfulness and obedience. Considerations as to consequences, even if they may have entered in at an earlier stage, no longer seem to be relevant. Indeed, as in the deep awareness of love, prudential criteria appear almost offensive. "Though he slay me, yet will I trust him" expresses more truly the cry of the heart. It is this fact which makes a theology of rewards and punishments so "off-putting" to sensitive minds.

In the light of this kind of experience some Christians have put forward another ethical view, over against the realist one, the intention being to do more justice to this strong sense of encounter and commitment. It may be briefly stated as follows.

Jesus uniquely reveals the divine purpose for men, and uniquely communicates divine power. In him, God takes the initiative and acts in a decisive and saving manner. Though history may be perplexingly difficult to interpret and often assumes the appearance of a veritable maze (sometimes a jungle), yet in Jesus faith finds God at work, fighting a cosmic battle against the forces of evil. What Christ did in his incarnate life, his follower is required to do in and through him. The believer has to wage an equally constant warfare against the evil in himself and in others. He will be successful only in so far as he does it through the strength and in the manner of his Lord— that is with the same weapons.

But how *did* Jesus conduct himself in the struggle? The answer (as we have seen in an earlier chapter) is that his was an intensely personalistic and sacrificial way, which fulfilled itself on a Cross. Thus the believer, as he commits himself to his Lord, experiences a similar constraint to follow along the same road. What this means, in practice, the believer will discover existentially in particular situations. Perhaps it is not inappropriate here to quote Albert Schweitzer:

"He comes to us as one unknown, without a name, as of old by the lake side He came to those men who knew Him not. He speaks to us the same word: 'Follow thou me', and sets us to the same task which He has to fulfil for our time. He commands. And to those who obey Him, whether they be wise or simple, He will reveal Himself in the toils, the conflicts, the sufferings which they shall pass through in His fellowship, and as an ineffable mystery, they shall learn in their own experience who He is."

This "way" may appear, externally assessed, "foolishness", a "stumbling block" to those with rigid categories of thought, but the initiate sees it as releasing power. The Christian's task, therefore, is simply one of obedience in a faith commitment; in the same way as the creative artist must be true to the "givenness" of his insight. The Christian does not *begin* by asking what is likely to happen if he acts in the sacrificial way of his Lord. Indeed he might maintain, with Farmer, that such a judgement of the natural reason is bound to leave out of account the very "fact" which constrains him—God's Providence at work within the total situation in which he is included. Rather when the Christian reflects on his actions he is more likely to ask himself whether what he did was in fact expressive of the way and the mind of Jesus. Has he been faithful? And this question will constitute a greater preoccupation than the embarking upon a nice assessment of possible consequences.

True it is, of course, that he is bound to believe that God will somehow most powerfully use this kind of dedication since it is in harmony with the way that God Himself chooses to work. But how God does this is His affair.

Such a conviction, and it is important to say this, does not mean that God will disdain to use other kinds of commitment which are not equally true to this ethic. Origen believed that He did. All that is asserted is that He can more effectively use that which moves in line with the highly particular way of Jesus—and that this cultivation ought to be the Christian's especial loyalty. What this dedication demands in concrete situations, no one can fully say in advance. It is when we get to them that we can know. It led Jesus finally to a Cross, and for his followers crucifixion at other levels, and in less dramatic a form, cannot be ruled out.

As Dibelius wrote: "For (Christians) there is no absolutely binding static doctrines of values or goods, or virtues. God speaks ever afresh to men by bringing them into new situations . . . the believer must constantly ask himself afresh: What is required of me here and now as a Christian?"

What *is* asserted is that this way is personal through and through. It entails relating ourselves to our brother men as persons, and not as things. It means encouraging in them a free response, respecting their particularity, and eschewing behaviour patterns which are so indiscriminate in their nature (even allowing for inevitable "adjustment" and "accommodation") as in no sense whatever to be capable of expressing Christ's way—indeed are in open violence to it.

Various criticisms have of course been brought against this view which I have just stated—that in practice it ends up by being pietistically escapist, and so on. It has been asserted that, in the sphere of the collective life, the personal content in human behaviour cannot always be one hundred per cent. vis-à-vis particular people; and that an absolutely personal ethic is, almost in the nature of the case, unattainable (in a world where some people do not behave as persons), even when the will to achieve it is present. For example, a Christian judge, presiding over an assize court and anxious to be true to a truly personal ethic, finds himself caught up on the horns of a dilemma. No overall pattern of law can, in respect of every individual, deal with him as a unique person, for it must take account of the total life of the community and in this respect be general in character. No matter how much, in its implementation, it is adjusted to meet particular situations, it cannot be fully "just", let alone "loving" to the offender in the dock. The "reasonable man" may be a necessary presupposition of any workable legal system, but like wisdom "where shall he be found?" The most that a group of scholars recently felt able to say about the concept of natural law was that it represented the idea that "the good is to be done and the evil avoided".[1]

It might be maintained that the impersonality of law relates itself to men only in their capacity as members of a collective system, and in this aspect of their total life ministers to them— but this I think would be too optimistic a view.

It can be replied, however, that there are behaviour patterns in which the personal confrontation is so minimal, indeed negated, that the Christian committed to a personal ethic must feel that he can have none of it. The refusal is particularly difficult for him when the behaviour pattern is not one of individual but community decision (such as an act of war) for this raises other and severe problems. Yet in spite of this, I think the Christian would be right to hold, to put it crudely, that there are actions which so outrage and violate what he believes to be true as to the nature of the real (the life of God) and consequently of

[1] It is for this reason that I felt bound to exclude considerations of natural law from this book since its foundations seem precarious.

effective personal relations, that no tension of a community loyalty can persuade him actively to take part in them. Such a form of behaviour, he believes, offers resistance to the working of the divine will, and as such (even though God will still endeavour to work within this continuum) he ought not to be engaged in it.

Precisely where to draw the line between the just acceptable and the wholly unacceptable demands great sensitivity and discernment, and different Christians will doubtless draw it differently. The making of moral judgements is not a science, and there are no propositions which can be applied by rule of thumb. It is more an art which demands an adult and responsible maturity. The person everlastingly asking, in personal affairs, "where do you draw the line?", and seeking some normative reply, has not yet travelled very far. Cut and dried answers to deep moral problems are not usually available. What the Church has to do is to proclaim the principles underlying such decisions.

For some Christians, and usually those whose ethical view tends to place the main emphasis on commitment, modern war comes under the category of the wholly unacceptable. The precise grounds for holding this view will vary, but substantially the rationale (if this is the right word) is the same. Modern war is so wholly indiscriminate, utterly non-personal, and absolutely destructive, that it must be seen as not simply somewhat removed from, but completely at variance with, the ethics of the Kingdom and incompatible with commitment to Jesus. Indeed it denies the relevance of such an ethic, which ought to become more relevant when the challenge against it is most severe. The question is never whether a Christian, within his commitment, may or may not use force, for he necessarily does this every day of his life: but what qualities of force may he use, upon whom, and when. The criterion for the Christian is that such force as he uses (mental, spiritual and physical) must be capable of being brought within some overall personal context.

There are difficulties in the ethical views which I have outlined above, and I hope I have been fair to both, though I myself am drawn to that of commitment. In the practical ordering of their lives, most Christians veer from placing the emphasis now on the one, now on the other. If the over-riding concern of the realist view is to be effective, that of the other is to be faithful. If the former weighs consequences, the latter cultivates insight. The former view claims to be more realistic, to face up to the resistances which the collective life offers to the establishment of the Kingdom. It claims in practice to get more done, and by accepting human nature for what it is makes it more nearly what it ought to be. It is suspicious of any idealism which generates a great deal of uplift, but somehow or other doesn't seem to be very effective in bringing the ideal down to earth. It is deeply concerned to accept personal responsibility for the course of events and to get Christians involved. It urges them to get to know the facts, do their homework and be practical. It wishes to encourage them when they are naturally disappointed at the poverty of their own achievement.

The other view places the primary emphasis on commitment to the way of Jesus, and all that this dedication presupposes in the realm of the personal life. Indeed it seeks to insist that people always act in a personal context. It denies that the ethics of the Kingdom are only applicable to the more intimate relations of life, but sees them, through faith, as capable of being introduced into the collective. The task of the Christian, finally, is not to reason why, but to do and if need be to die. Consequences may be safely left to God's providential care. To quote Dr. H. H. Farmer again: "In the last resort it is God's business to preserve human life and whatever is indispensable to it: it is our business to do His will, committing everything else to Him." Man lives in God's world: and an excessive preoccupation and anxiety with the consequences flowing from human action, particularly when we remember the complexity and the limitations involved in the nature of the judgement, seem to be lacking in faith and trust. It is like a man weighing up the pros and cons in friendship. If the Way of Jesus is a divinely revealed way, might this not mean that human life at its highest levels, that is in pursuit of the "ends" which God set himself in creation, will only move to fulfilment this way; and may it not be that God can save equally by many as by few? Does not the whole life of Jesus and the sharpness of His dedication bear this out?

At least such a view does allow a specifically Christian conscience to be true to itself, and not be forced to overcome its own scruples in the process of action. Is it hopelessly naïve, for example, for the follower of Jesus to place the hydrogen bomb alongside the Cross, and to see the one as the complete and absolute antithesis of the other?

As I said when I first entered upon this discussion, these two ethical views hardly seem to come to grips with each other. They start at different ends, and both obviously have something to say to the Christian, and bear a necessary witness, in a world where human insights are partial and men "see through a glass darkly". The Christian needs the challenge of involvement and commitment for the building up of the Kingdom. Maybe in the ordinary world of everyday discipleship we weigh consequences: in the great crises of life we enter a more immediate world of final encounter and constraint. I myself would place the final emphasis on the latter.

In suggesting an eclectic or reconciling attitude to these two approaches I feel some scruples as I do so, in so far as they may tend to create different behaviour patterns, not only in the intimacies of personal relations—this is to be expected—but also in the paterns of collective behaviour where a greater order is needed. The danger inherent in the realist view is that in its endeavour to be rationally practical it can quite cease to be Christian: in the other that by placing its whole emphasis on existential living and personal commitment it may introduce conflicting patterns into the collective life and hardly stand for a recognisable moral order. Can this dilemma be overcome by an appeal to specialised vocation, which finds room for both individual commitment to the Kingdom, and also for more normative patterns essential to the life of the community? Dr. William Temple thought that it could.

During the last war, he had to wrestle with the problem of the pacifist-non-pacifist dilemma. For himself he believed that the war against Nazi Germany must be fought and won, and he had no hesitation in saying so. Yet at the same time he believed that God placed a special and genuine vocation of pacifism on some Christians, just in order that during the clash of arms, with its inevitable defilement, witness might still be made to that Kingdom whose fruits are love, joy and peace.

This is an attractive view, for if one could but hold it some of the difficulties to which I have called attention, if they do not disappear, at least seem less acute.

Yet candour compels me to ask whether its presuppositions are not open to question; and whether in fact it does justice to either party. When a man feels a vocation to the religious life, he recognises that the compulsion is personal to himself. He would not for a moment think that every other man ought to be in his position. Is this equally true of the constraint to pacifism or non-pacifism? It seems doubtful. A man enduring the horrors of war, and sustained only by the conviction that it is imperative to fight it, recognises, as a possibility, that he may be mistaken in taking this stand: but he believes that he is not, and, though he respects the conscience of those who do not stand with him, he yet regards this conscience as uninformed. Precisely the same is true the other way round, in respect of the pacifist, though in view of his ethic of commitment he might find it a little more difficult to sustain his position in argument. In fact, however, most pacifists do not only say: "Here I stand": but also "This is where the followers of Jesus ought to stand".

It may be said that both parties go too far in making this further claim—but that they do make it I think there can be little doubt. Perhaps this derives from a deep and ultimate conviction that there is a moral order, personal though it may be: and that the Spirit does not constrain people to mutually hostile patterns of behaviour. To do so seems like using some people as a means to another's end. Though God deals with each man in his existential situation—that is within the context of his own life—yet the body of Christ cannot finally be an organism in which, at one level, there is war between its members. "Can both walk together unless they be agreed?"

I leave this dilemma unresolved—perhaps it is incapable of resolution—trusting in the larger hope that God will use all honest inclinations to seek His will. I stress the problem only because I think there is a complacent tendency in contemporary moral theology, and equally in more popular thought, to use such phrases as "a tension of opposites", "polarity", "dialectic", "ambiguity"—and so on. I fear I myself have not avoided the temptation. Such terms can easily encourage the suggestion (though this is not the intention) that there is a certain profundity in holding together what seem mutually exclusive truths. In this context we must be careful to distinguish between the "tension" which conceals lazy and loose thinking—that is an inability to make up our minds, or a desire to have the best of both worlds—from the "tension" which results from the richness of man's experience of God, and the consequent inadequacy of our "thought categories" to contain it. The latter springs from the nature of the divine-human encounter—and the supreme mystery of God.

But not all ethical problems move in this kind of world. Whether a man ought to be judicially hanged by the neck: whether a hydrogen bomb ought ever to be dropped, or a race segregated—these are not questions in respect of which an excessive amount of ambiguity is always helpful. A Christian opinion which, in these matters, is divided from top to bottom will not command the influence which it should.

Such reflections can of course be dangerous. They lay themselves open to the misunderstanding that there ought to be one authoritative Christian opinion authoritatively proclaimed—which the whole of this book, in some respects, is an appeal against. Or it might even suggest an intolerance of minority opinion, which ought equally to be deplored.

My concern is to make a protest against a too facile, too easy, and far too complacent acceptance of differences in a Christian moral witness; in particular in those areas of conduct which concern the collective life and where unambiguous action needs to be taken. Christians ought to wish to come to a common mind on matters of great social and political urgency. When discipleship of the same Lord leads to very different social and political policies, some of them mutually exclusive, the man in the street, unaware perhaps of the complexities involved, is inclined to exclaim: "A plague on both your houses." And who can blame him?

The Christian Church has often been far too long and far too timid in defining its view, and this has not always been due either to the complexity of the existing situation or a sensitivity to minority opinion. What untold suffering and future antagonisms might have been avoided if the Christian Churches had been able *earlier* to condemn, in forthright terms, the iniquitous slave trade? The same may prove to be true of contemporary apartheid, in respect of which unanimity (more or less) has come very late in the day.

V: MAINLY PSYCHOLOGICAL

CHAPTER IX

(a) CONSCIENCE

So FAR, WITH the exception of the previous chapter, Christian ethics have been treated in the main historically. It is now time, in these last chapters, to see them from a slightly different point of view, to bring together some of the thoughts suggested earlier—and to be practical. It is a basic contention in this book that what Christian Ethics are about can only be understood against the background of Christian Faith.

Ethics have been described as "the science of morals or duty". To put this even more simply, they have to do with conduct, with how people behave—or ought to behave—and the motives which lie behind their behaviour.

That distinctions of right and wrong are made, no matter how explained or explained away, is a fact of common everyday experience. All societies throw up behaviour patterns, and surround them with sanctions of one kind or another. These patterns customarily evoke the psychological compulsion of "oughtness", quite independently of external penalties imposed upon the man who breaks them. Indeed it is not easy to see how external punishments could evoke the sense of "oughtness"; which is something quite different from a sense of fear: or an anticipation of disagreeable consequences.

The Christian Faith is prepared to give real (metaphysical) significance to the moral experience of mankind: and to see it as bound up with man's essential status in the universe as an accountable person.

In this respect, though not in other respects, Emmanuel Kant, the celebrated German philosopher—of whom it has been said that he enjoyed the unique advantage over his successors of never having had to study Emmanuel Kant—may be taken as representative of the Christian position. Kant regarded the moral experience of man as revelatory of what it finally means to be a person. For the most part, he maintains, man in his experience of the world is caught up only in phenomena, that is in appearances: of the noumenal, that is the thing in itself, he knows nothing. In the moral intuition, however, he penetrates to the very heart of reality, within himself and without. Every man in certain situations says "I ought", and this psychological response is unique. If we enquire as to the precise nature of this experience, we run into difficulty, although it is certain we cannot explain it away in other terms. "I ought" does not mean "I find pleasure in" or "I am compelled to". It simply and uniquely means "I ought" and this experience of inner constraint brings with it a sense of absolute obligation. Whether I shall in fact do what I feel I ought to do is another matter. What I know, or more accurately, what is given to me in the experience of "oughtness", is what Kant described as a "categorical imperative". Doubtless in some men this is more highly developed than in others; and the obligation may register itself around diverse patterns of behaviour in various societies at different stages of development. Kant's argument, however, is not affected by these obvious facts. What he basically affirms is that all people necessarily know, from their own immediate experience, what "oughtness" is, simply because they are living, and necessarily so, as human beings. If they do *not* know, nobody can explain it to them, any more than a man born blind can explain to another what colour is. In his moral experience man steps out of the phenomenal world into the noumenal: and it is because of this that Kant, after having destroyed, as he thought, the traditional arguments for God's existence, uses the moral experience to reinstate it.

Christians, of course, by no means all assent to the philosophy of Emmanuel Kant. He has been quoted merely in the limited context of the moral experience because he so strongly calls attention to the fact that ethical behaviour results from man's experience of "oughtness"; and that this experience indicates that man is no self-sufficient arbiter of his own destiny. He is accountable to God; a steward who must render up an account. "Rightness is the replacement of egoism by the voluntary acceptance of the rule of God." That is to say, the Christian interprets the voice of what is popularly termed the conscience as due to the pressure of another reality upon him—the reality of God. In all moral action man's will seeks and responds (though not necessarily perfectly) to the divine will. Although in this respect the "value" apprehended in moral experience is objective—for God is external to man in the sense that he is transcendent as well as immanent—it is yet subjectively known in concrete situations.

Does this mean that there is an objective moral code, in the same way as there are uniformities (laws) discoverable in the physical universe, which all men must necessarily respect?

If the Christian is prepared to answer a question of this kind, which he would probably regard as wrongly put, he would reply both "yes" and "no". "No", in so far as a Christian ethic does not mean adherence to a rigid propositional morality, but sets out to discover in particular situations "what the will of the Lord is". "Yes", in so far as in acting morally the Christian believes himself to be responding to an absolute Reality. Indeed, it is this conviction which can give such high resolution to his moral endeavour and enable him to stand an "Athanasius against the world". It frees him from the tyranny of earthly forces outside himself, and from unregenerate impulses within himself which would make him a slave. In the last analysis, that which is right does not derive its rightness, and hence its authority, from the fact that man's will seeks it, or from an external human authority which propounds it, but from God's sovereignty over His universe.

This truth has obvious practical implications. Thus it is not the force with which governments support justice which gives to justice its claim and sanction: nor does the sanction derive from the collective will of society. It is to God's will finally that all things in Heaven and earth are subject—ruler as well as ruled. Justice is that which God, in this situation, decrees, though (as will be suggested later) His is no arbitrary decree, since in God supreme power and absolute value are one.

It is important at this stage, however, to make it clear that the view above stated has no necessary connection with the way in which moral judgements are arrived at; the mechanism, as it were, of the psychological processes leading up to them. Doubtless it is the total environment, physical, psychical, spiritual (if such distinctions may for convenience be allowed)—the society in which man lives—that constitutes the womb within which God works to bring to birth moral judgements in man—that is works to fulfil persons. What matters is not so much the nurture, but the nature of the judgement implied in the moral experience. It is only because man has the potential to develop into a moral person that his environment is able to evoke a particular moral response. What the Christian may well find it difficult to accept is that the pressure of society which conditions men to regard certain behaviour patterns as right and others as wrong also generates the capacity to make the distinction. To assert this would be to go too far, though doubtless it is helpful to be reminded that man is a social animal, and (as Joseph Butler maintained) that altruism, or concern for others, is as fundamental and natural to man as is concern for himself. This is not surprising since the original unit of society was not an isolated self. The consciousness of being a unique person only comes to exist through the relationship of self to not-self: and this relationship is prior to the subsequent differentiation. The baby is aware of its mother, not as opposed to, but as part of, his awareness of himself. The individual becomes fully personal only within the group.

The Christian, then, is prepared to take the conscience, or moral experience, seriously, and to regard it as a significant indication that man lives and moves and has his being under the sovereignty and the judgement of God. True the conscience (as we have seen) does not operate in a vacuum, but within the given situations in which men live from day to day. God deals with people in the "here and now" and as they are. The experience of "oughtness" is not a diffused awareness or a vague sense of a general duty. It registers obligation in a particular context, prompting men to do or not to do certain things; or more accurately it adds or introduces a sense of obligation to the doing or avoiding of certain acts.

Yet it is no part of Christian teaching that the conscience is infallible. A man's conscience, in so far as it moves him to act in a particular way, may be in error; it may be uninstructed; it may be in a position of almost culpable ignorance. Such a condition makes it the more difficult for God, who does not obliterate persons in the moral experience but seeks to elicit a free response, to work within it. Often the highest response which He can evoke, if He is to respect a man's integrity—and He must do this for there can be no morality without such respect—is far removed from an absolute ethical position. As such, it bears painful witness to the moral situation in which a man at present is, but it constitutes (for him) a step forward. The creaturely nature of man makes him only too prone to mistake his own interests for the "good" and to moralise his instinctive urges.

E

The collective (as every debate in U.N.O. plainly illustrates) is always self-justifying, and never admits error.

Yet fallible though the conscience may be, a man must follow it. If he does not, he has done violence to what is most sacred within himself. He has not only "missed the mark" but he has committed rebellion against God.

It is just here that the Christian conviction as to the objective reference of conscience helps him, though it is this fact, of course, which constitutes a problem to the enquiring mind. It was this deep conviction, for example, which supported Luther before the German Diet, as he stood his ground. Superior physical force might commit him to death or imprisonment, but he dare not voluntarily act against his own conscience. "We must obey God rather than man" has often served to rally a noble man, and the God he thus serves is revealed through the intimations of his own conscience. Martyrs on the scaffold (no matter what their religious commitment) in practice regard the "moral intuition" (to use F. H. Bradley's phrase) as ultimate, that is as possessing a unique claim upon them which just cannot be disregarded. The Christian martyr goes even further and is convinced that finally the strong arm of Eternity is behind him, and that the absolute sense of obligation which he experiences is none other than a divine constraint.

There is then a seeming contradiction which cannot, in pure discursive thought, be resolved. The conscience is authoritative in that when it finally registers itself, it must be obeyed; yet objective though its reference may be, it does not register to an absolute ethic from which a universally valid moral code can be deduced. The pressure to act in a certain way; the sense of obligation around a particular pattern of conduct—these represent the pressure of the Spirit of God upon men, but mediated through an actual situation. Thus though it is "right" for men to respond to this pressure, it may still not represent a fully developed pattern of ethical behaviour. Within *this man's* particular situation in space and time, given *his* life history up to date, it would be wrong for him not to act as his conscience prompts (though in extreme situations the state may have to restrain him in the exercise of it); but this is not necessarily to say that he ought to be in this position.

The fact is, I repeat, that God does not obliterate people even when He enters into relations with them. They do not become merely instruments. He deals with them within the context of their personal life, and insight is bestowed within their given situation. St. Paul realistically recognised this limitation when he discusses the attitude which Christians ought to take to the eating of meat previously offered to idols. He admits that the Kingdom of God is not eating and drinking, and that a mature Christian is free of such taboos. Yet he urges restraint, since to encourage a "tender (i.e. undeveloped) conscience" to offend against its own standards is to lead a brother into sin.

Uninformed though a conscience may be, it still merits respect, though this does not mean that no attempt should be made to enlighten it.

To summarise: conscience does not operate in a vacuum. It is not a diffused awareness that there is such a thing as the divine will; but it is a concrete experience arising out of a particular set of conditions. God's will is known through a call to definite action. Here the personalistic philosophy of Christianity is peculiarly relevant, for it is basic to its view that God deals with persons as persons, respecting their integrity. The divine constraint to action is never absolutely coercive: it can be, and often is, resisted, though the result of such resistance, paradoxically, is the weakening of final freedom in man, for freedom itself must be understood within the terms of man's final nature and destiny. "Cui servare est regnare", or as Cranmer, with a touch of genius, translated these words: "Whose service is perfect freedom."

(b) TELOS

All ethical patterns ultimately assume an "end" or "telos" which is supremely valuable—that is they move towards some conception of the good life. If we can talk of a communist ethic, it would mean an ethic, or pattern of behaviour, which promotes the ends which communism sets out to realise. For the Christian, man's chief end, to quote the impressive opening words of the Shorter Catechism of the Presbyterian Church, is "to glorify God and to enjoy Him for ever". That is intrinsically valuable which both assists this end and is the experience of it. A man perfectly glorifying God is a man perfectly fulfilled. The end and the means to it are one and the same thing.

The Christian enters into this telos by cultivating that mind which was in Christ Jesus, since Christ himself glorified God by effectively performing His will. The telos for man, by God's grace, is to be "raised to the measure of the stature of the fullness of Christ" and that measure is expressed in his petition in the Garden of Gethsemane: "Not as I will but as thou wilt". In the Lord's prayer, which he taught his disciples, absolute priority is given to the hallowing of God's name, and the building up of His Kingdom. The presupposition is that through this dedication a man fully becomes himself. As St. Augustine puts it: "Thou Lord God hast made us for thyself; and our hearts shall never find rest until they rest in Thee." So it is that a man is fulfilled by giving glory to God in the perfect obedience of a son—and ethical behaviour is that which leads to this end and is the realisation of it.

Once again we are confronted by a paradox. It is only through selfgiving, through renunciation, that a man "arrives", and this "arrival" for the Christian means commitment to Christ as Lord. This commitment has positive and formative content. In the Gospels we read of the impact of the historic Jesus upon the first disciples, and of the quality of life which discipleship involves. It is one of Christ-likeness, within the basic structure of each man's particularity—that is it, does not mean a slavish copying of Jesus but a realisation of God's will through entering into the spirit of his sacrificial life. This kind of virtue is one of ordering personal relationships in such a way as to have an absolute respect for the other person as himself uniquely made to give God glory. We must not treat another man as a *thing* for our own convenience, a means whereby we realise our own private and self-regarding ends. We must not try to condition him, to manipulate, to use him, in order to impose our wills upon him as we would do with a machine, thereby securing a response which is most convenient to us. We must not try to compensate for our personal failures by being aggressive against others. To treat another person as uniquely made for God demands in us a high degree of imaginative understanding, the more so as we must endeavour to see him in his existential situation. "Don't do to others as you would that they should do unto you", said Bernard Shaw. "Their tastes may not be the same." What the Christian seeks is to see the other person as linked with himself in a community whose individual and corporate life exist to offer to God "the honour due unto His Name". The end is a kingdom of fulfilled persons.

Given such a basic pattern of personal commitment, the resulting ethic cannot hope to be precise and formal. To convert it into a set of rigid commandments cannot be done without impairing its inner structure. Essentially it is a dynamic, purposeful ethic resolving itself in given situations. Its cultivation is more a matter of insight and imagination than of precise deduction from a moral absolute. Thus it is difficult for a Christian to discuss moral problems in a vacuum without taking account of the rich particularity in which all moral situations are involved: though the intention is always to behave towards others in such a way as to help them to become more truly persons.

It is important, however, to sound a cautionary note at this point. To insist that to act ethically is to act in conformity with the will of God (so as to give Him glory) does not mean that the Christian obeys a dictate of mere power. God, who is the source of all existence, the fount of all energy, is also the source and sustainer of value. Indeed He is the supremely valuable. To do God's will is to do the "good".

(c) MOTIVE

The will of God—so the teaching of Jesus and Christian experience across the centuries would seem to suggest—is not directed towards eliciting a static perfection, but is concerned to promote a purposeful growth, which persists even beyond death. Various ethical systems set themselves different ends, that is entertain different conceptions of the "good". For example, some philosophers, though not many, have suggested that the chief practical end for man is to enter into a state of happiness; and consequently that that conduct is right which promotes the greatest happiness of the greatest number. Such hedonism, though in certain situations it constitutes a good practical guide to conduct (and it certainly did so in England when Bentham, the great utilitarian, advocated it) breaks down on a more detailed examination as when it is suggested that one man should give up his own happiness for another. It is difficult to be consistently quantitative about happiness—to add it up: but once "quality" or "grade" is introduced as a criterion, that is, differences between one kind of happiness and another, the whole case for a systematic hedonism collapses. John Stuart Mill recognised this and recanted so far from orthodox utilitarianism as to maintain: "Better be Socrates dissatisfied than a pig satisfied."

Happiness is but one among many ends which have been suggested as the goal of moral effort. Others are "the harmonious person", "the perfect realisation of function", "the loss of individuality", "reverence for life", "herrenvolk", and so on. The Christian end has been stated already as the glorifying of God by commitment to Jesus. Its final validity, and the ethical system which promotes it, must rest, I suspect, upon the metaphysical truth of the Christian claim that its picture of Ultimate Reality is a true one.

If to do good is to obey God's will, it is important to say again that this obedience perfects a man and makes him free, in the same way as the artist, who is master of his craft and has learnt its techniques, becomes free in respecting them. He finds the forms to which he is subject no strait-jacket, but the means to his own liberation, the conditions within which he must work in order to be true to the best in himself and to the given.

But candour compels me to ask how far the motive of glorifying God by doing His will can constitute a *conscious* incentive (or motive) to action. No one will deny that right motive is an essential element in a fully articulated right action. Kant consistently maintained that the only thing that was wholly good was a good will: and T. S. Eliot reminds us that "the supreme treason is to do the right thing for the wrong reason." Indeed it is often the motive which, superficially at least, seems to give to the action, or rather to the person doing the action, rightness or wrongness. To kill an animal to get it out of intolerable pain is one thing: to kill it out of petty annoyance, for amusement or sheer blood lust is quite another. They move in altogether different worlds of morality, though the physical act may be performed in precisely the same manner.

Of course motives seldom exist in a pure form. Usually the

motives prompting to action are mixed, some of which might loosely be described as "worthy", others as "not so worthy". One of the lessons that modern psychiatry has taught us is that motivation is a very complex affair, and is by no means confined to the conscious mind. Often there are drives to action which are hidden deep in the subconscious, and which derive in part from our life history—or even from the history of the race. We do well, therefore, to be somewhat suspicious when we tend to be over-confident as to the purity or rectitude of our motives. It is obviously important that our motives should be as high as we can contrive to make them: but to be over-curious or precious about them is often to be self-defeating, as St. Paul found in his early and moralistic days. We have already seen, at the other extreme, how Christian ethics in the eighteenth century were cheapened and depraved by seeking to base them upon a rationalistic hedonism. It was in protest against such a perversion that Butler preached his famous Rolls sermons. Many eighteenth-century theologians would have done better to ask themselves whether the reward for goodness can ever be other than more goodness. Jesus, in the Gospels, places the emphasis elsewhere than in the returns which goodness brings. He sees morality as springing from a filial response of man to God his Father, and he condemns unworthy motives as corrupting what might otherwise be worth-while action. "When thou doest thine alms, do not sound a trumpet before thee, as the hypocrites do in the synagogues and in the streets, that they may have glory of men. Verily, I say unto you, they have their reward."

Thus it is that Christianity asserts that finally the highest goodness flows from the worshipful response—that is from the recognition of the intrinsic "worth" of God as Himself "supremely valuable". Such alone constitutes a valid and true rationale for morality. The reasons for this transcendentalism may be briefly stated.

In our relations with our fellow men, it is impossible (both in theory and practice) for some element of wrongful self-love or introversion not to enter in so long as these personal relationships constitute a closed system. No human love, for example, is potentially higher or more self-denying than that of a mother for her own children. Yet even in her selfless devotion she can never absolutely rid herself of self-love, since there is something of herself in the child, who in his early years is absolutely dependent upon her. Such a situation obtains, in greater and less degrees, in all human relations. It is simply part of man's predicament; and the necessary result is to make it the more difficult fully to respect the integrity of others. Something of possessiveness, something of self-assertion, will inevitably creep in.

But God is not dependent upon us in the same way: we are not necessary to make up his perfection. Within His own Being, there is everything necessary to the fullness of His Divine Life. God is the Creator: we are His creatures. Thus it follows that man, in recognising the worth of the divine ground, enters into a relation which, from the human side, is alone capable of being freed from introversion and self-regard. In this relation, he can be free and freed, being made aware of the supreme value as supremely valuable, and knowing within himself that he cannot condition or manipulate this reality for his own ends. True the temptation to do so may all too often be present (how much petitionary prayer bears witness to this endeavour!) but its intrinsic absurdity is self-evident, for the relationship is unique. To seek to use God is to descend into magic.

Thus the ultimate motivation lying behind Christian conduct has a Godward reference, though this does not necessarily mean that the experienced or conscious motive in every concrete situation is to glorify God. To say that it is would be an affectation. The Christian recognises that a man cannot serve God, whom he has not seen, unless he serves his brother man whom he has seen. The limited horizon, with its obvious calls and challenges, demands his full attention. One step at a time is good enough for him. He is grateful that there are worshipful and significant occasions when this general recognition is brought to self-consciousness and heightened awareness; when he sees that whatever sacrifical living he has achieved is part of his offering to the Father God.

The distinction which has been made above is by no means an irrelevant "piosity". There *is* a difference between a morality which ends up by being moralistic and self-regarding (though this may not be its original intention), which sees or uses other people merely as a means through which by serving them we become good: and a morality which ultimately interprets all right action as a response to divine grace, and an offering due to the God of all holiness and love—the self-subsistent ground of all value. The latter reference relieves goodness of some of the unattractiveness, some of the sanctimoniousness, which can unfortunately all too easily go along with it. The children's prayer: "O God make the nice people good and the good people nice" may have some point in this context. One is reminded of the well-known gibe of Macaulay that the Puritans disliked bear baiting, not because of the pain it inflicted on the animals, but because of the pleasure it gave the spectators.

To give God the glory offers more scope and range for the developing spirit of man. Such an end is capable of including within its act of dedication all the rich and sacramental varieties of human experience. It moves in a world beyond morality.

(d) POWER

In Chapter V, when dealing with St. Paul, reference was made to the fact that the ethical problem is not simply one of know-ledge. Of course there is much truth in the contention (the

Buddha and Socrates thought so) that the tragedy of human life is more that people mistake what goodness is rather than that they do not seek it. If only they *really* knew where it is to be found, if they could but see it shining with its own clear light, then they would inevitably be drawn to it, and the more easily follow it. The recognition, which involves the experiencing of value, would incline the will towards it. Virtue *is* knowledge. As Tennyson wrote: "We needs must love the highest when we see it"—but how seldom we effectively *do* see it.

There is, I repeat, truth here, particularly if by "seeing goodness" we mean being made aware of its intrinsic nature. Jesus always recognised that there was an element of sheer ignorance in sin. "Father forgive them for they know not what they do." This was not simply a piece of charitable sentimentality but the mere statement of a fact. Many of the actors in this tragic event *did not* know what they were doing. "In ignorance ye did it", said St. Peter. There is undoubtedly a great deal of unadulterated lack of knowledge in sin, though the condition of ignorance is often highly culpable. Sometimes, indeed, it is of so deep-seated a kind that it becomes impossible for the ignorant man to recognise vice and virtue for what they are. His understanding is darkened, and he needs to be taught virtue.

What has just been said refers to a lack of knowledge which may be described as a form of moral blindness. We are all, in varying degrees, afflicted by it. There is, however, another kind of ignorance which comes from not knowing the relevant facts within which the moral judgement has to be made. An existential ethic, such as the Christian undoubtedly is, needs to be peculiarly sensitive to real situations. A good will without the necessary homework is not enough! Indeed where such mental laziness exists the goodness of the will may well be questioned.

In this double sense of adequate insight and the need for factual information knowledge is essential to virtue. To practise it is a skill. Psychological awareness, sensitivity to people—these are necessary for its fuller realisation. A man who intends to do good, but who ends up by increasing the area in which evil operates, can only with great reservations be regarded as a good man. The path to hell is often paved with good intentions, and to mean well is sometimes rightly regarded as a term of reproach.

It would be idle to pretend, however, that the moral problem can be exhausted in this way. It is not only ignorance which stands in between a man and virtue. The will often proves itself to be irresolute, even rebellious, and men lack power to do the good, even though they desire it. As St. Paul says in a piece of autobiographical writing: "The good that I would I do not: but the evil which I would not that I do."

The ethical problem cannot be meaningfully discussed from a Christian angle without taking into account this psychological or spiritual condition. Man needs to be instructed: but he just as urgently needs to be rescued and set free—in theological language to be redeemed. He needs help (grace) to live the good life—an active infusion of power.

Since man's moral responses are significant in his life-history, sin must be taken seriously. Man is accountable to God and made for "virtue" (using this word in its fullest possible connotation) and therefore no personal condition can be more destructive of the psyche than that which can result from the past catching up with us—that is from the effects and sometimes the consciousness of sin unforgiven.

The phrase a "guilt complex" was not first coined in religious circles but in the psychological clinics of central Europe: and though the psychiatrist may deal therapeutically with this condition by seeking to dispel it—that is by bringing it into the light of consciousness and then explaining it away—he is yet vividly aware of its serious, almost deadly effects. Such a psychological state can breed the most serious neuroses, leading at times to an almost dramatic collapse of the person. The Christian sees these breakdowns as distortions, or perversions, of a real situation. Sin, unconfessed and unforgiven, can work havoc in the psyche, like a cancer festering unknown to its victim, at levels lower than his conscious awareness of it. Sin means separation. It is the love impulse gone wrong. Thus it is that a Christian ethic cannot be discussed, or understood, apart from this psychological condition, which means apart from the grace of God. The Christian needs to experience the curative effects resulting from the divine forgiveness, and to cultivate techniques of power. There is no need to wallow in sin, that is to become morbidly introspective, in order to recognise the creative leap forward which can set in upon the conscious "renewing of love".

The Christian pattern of Christ-like virtue is livable only as men wait upon God in penitence, in prayer and in worship. It is because of this that there is a distinction (I believe there are other distinctions as well) between a humanist and a Christian ethic. True, nothing is more stupid, indeed more blasphemous, than to decry humanism. A man who truly is a humanist, who has a real concern and respect for his fellow men, and strives to serve them, is a good man indeed. The world needs more of them.

Yet it is not improper, or uncharitable, to notice a difference of emphasis. Christianity is not solely concerned with standards of ethical behaviour, but with the means of living up to them. It suggests that a liberated virtue the more effectively flourishes where a worshipful response is at the centre: where a man puts himself in the way of receiving divine grace: where the "end" that he seeks is understood as seeking him: and God is known as both demand and succour. The praise is His.

It is because of this truth that it is doubtful how far a vital and distinctive Christian ethic can survive when divorced from its energising source in the living God, and cut off from that Faith which proclaims and witnesses to belief in Him.

VI: MAINLY PRACTICAL

CHAPTER X

CHRISTIAN ETHICS AND CONTEMPORARY SOCIETY

A WELL-KNOWN COMEDIAN, in the course of his escapades, used to ask plaintively: "What's to do?" It is, in some respects, every man's question, and it is certainly one of the tasks of a great religion to serve as a guide to conduct, and to help people in their capacities as children and parents, as workers and citizens. People need guidance and suggestion: to be reminded of whatever norms there may be in the moral life. What they do not need, however, is for responsible decisions to be taken out of their hands.

We have seen the Christian Faith trying to provide such guidance, and though it is not a moralistic religion, yet it undoubtedly places an enormous emphasis on behaviour, and takes the conscience seriously. "Not every one that saith unto me Lord, Lord, shall enter into the Kingdom of Heaven, but he that doeth the will of my Father which is in Heaven." Christianity, however, simply because it is a dynamic faith, encouraging personal commitment and stressing the particularity of people— no one can be quite in another's shoes—does not easily lend itself to a statement of what that will is in propositional form.

But this individualism is not the whole story. Christianity places an equal (but not opposed) emphasis on the collective, both within its own community the Church, as the Body of Christ, and also within the nation or whatever the social unit happens to be. Christianity stands for freedom, the freedom of real people held together in a personal order, which is finally one of love. In its teaching the church endeavours, at one level, to interpret the will of God normatively, and to help its members by mediating to them a collective wisdom which has matured across the years. This means that God confronts the believer in his total situation as belonging to a community as well as in his solitariness.

Yet how does this help when it comes to dealing with specific matters of conduct, personal and corporate; and how does this stress on the divine-human encounter in its unique contexts avoid encouraging an individualism which ends with every man his own deity?

In reply to such understandable scruples, it is necessary to state that the Christian Faith has a great deal to say about the "orders" (to quote Luther's phrase) within which men necessarily live and "orders" demand an "order": but in so doing it insists that people be treated as adult and responsible. Intimate and personal affairs, and the ethical problems involved in them, do not always admit of a precise answer, and only the people who are within the total situation can really be sensitive to them. The final concern of the Christian is not to act normatively (advisable though this often is) but to endeavour to realise a life of sacrificial love. The rich particularity of the individual make-up, the uniqueness of every man's life history, the confrontation by God of persons in the situations where they are rather than where they ought to be—these often mean a response which is highly distinctive, so that what may be fitting (I decline to use the word "right") in *this* context and for *this* person may be at variance, in its objective expression, with what is fitting for other people in similar (but in fact *not* similar) situations. What finally matters is not the response seen from the outside, but the spirit of renunciation and sacrificial living which ought to inform, for the Christian, all his responses to existential situations. Where this exists there will in fact be an inclusive order. A human relationship in respect of which it is right that a particular external structure should be accepted as normative is not necessarily weakened because at times there are departures from it—that is departures from its external and practical expression. The normative is that which human nature tends to move towards and fulfil itself in: it represents the wisdom of a continuing collective experience. But nothing can be more disastrous than to pay it lip service but to offend its very spirit.

When it comes to the collective life, the follower of Jesus must of necessity be more concerned with common standards of behaviour. Here he will be wise to ask himself: if the picture of Ultimate Reality be as Christian Faith affirms that it is, what general principles of conduct would seem necessarily to result from it? Are there any absolutes which in their basic structure are unchanging and to which social life must conform? Is it possible, if the nature of man is as the Bible suggests him to be, to say something about necessary patterns of collective existence?

I myself believe that there are certain norms to which the Christian Faith gives its sanction and from which society departs at its peril: but the personal content in these will vary according to the particular "order" which expresses them. In saying this I do not wish to make a plea for a double standard since the Christian all the time has to live out his Faith in terms of a Christ-like committal, and in the obedience of a son. But I am claiming that though there must be norms, otherwise the community life would be anarchy (and God is a God of order), yet ultimately even the normative may have to give way to more personal needs. Finally the motivation to right conduct lies outside and beyond the scope of any formal law—whether it be of State or Church. The most that such law can hope to do is to suggest the road that a man would be wise to tread, but it can only take him a very small part of the way. Jesus was as much concerned with adultery in the heart and with evil thoughts that rise up from within as he was with external behaviour. It would be possible for a Christian to observe punctiliously the laws of Church and State, but there need be no love in the heart, no joy in the soul, and as a consequence no distinctive virtue.

So it follows that a Christian sociology, even if it could be enforced by external sanctions, would not be fully Christian for those who conform to it without a right disposition of the heart.

It is against this ambiguity that the following remarks are offered.

(II)

The Christian is to give glory to God through sacrificial Christ-like living, and for this to happen he must be rescued from sin and infused with power. Yet this does not answer the question how this distinctive quality or pattern of life fits into the total human situation in which Christians necessarily live their day-to-day lives, which situation they help to create. Yet no one can deny that Christianity, in releasing energies and encouraging commitment to living, has created the kind of problem which it has not been always able to solve. These problems are often so complex that there can be no one answer to them.

The main stream of Christian tradition has insisted that man is to glorify God here and now, and this means that he must do so within the framework of the "orders"—the "orders" being (in 1961) the family, the nation, the Church and (beyond 1961) whatever other "order" the changing life of man in society may throw up. Indeed we might enlarge the concept of the "orders" to include a man's work.

Some Christians have tended to see one or other of these orders as absolute, and to regard particular expressions of them as unalterable. Not only are they God-given but eternally constituted. Man is fulfilled by bringing himself into conformity with these absolutes, and to respect them is not to be imprisoned in a strait-jacket but to be liberated. Marriage, for example, conceived as a life-long relationship of a man to a woman to the exclusion of all other is such an absolute. The teaching of Jesus therefore has been interpreted as indicating almost a metaphysical relationship, incapable, during the lifetime of the partners, of destruction. Divorce is not simply precluded, it is impossible. It can neither end one marriage nor lead to another. The original unity must in the nature of the case remain.

Yet such a claim can become misleading, and indeed may not promote a personalistic ethic if it is pushed to extreme lengths. That the family seems a natural (and therefore?) God-ordained unit may for practical purposes be accepted: and there is great significance, for the Christian, in the fact that the metaphor of marriage for the covenant relationship of Yaweh with His people is frequently used in the Old Testament. Paul sees marriage as "signifying the mystical union that is betwixt Christ and his Church". Nor must it be forgotten that Jesus employs the language of home and family to introduce his hearers to the life of God, who is the supreme Father. Christian Faith gives great importance to the stability and integrity of the home and the security which this provides. It believes that it is here that particularity is sharpened and yet creatively held together in a community of love. In the family the problem of the one and the many is resolved at the personal level, and the opportunities for sacrificial living extended. Larger loyalties spring out of lesser. That Jesus himself saw marriage as fulfilling itself in a monogamous life-long relationship of love: and divorce as due to the "hardness of men's hearts", and in that sense sinful, there can, I think, be little doubt. To this the testimony and early practice of the Church bear witness. But to find here an absolute, in the sense that divorce is utterly precluded in any circumstances, is to suppose that we can both discover the very words of Jesus, and having discovered them, use them as authoritative in a particular way. To suppose that great moral (and intensely personal) questions can be settled by wrestling with texts, waiting upon the latest results of critical scholarship and the precise translation of a Greek word, is to make Jesus a legalist, morality propositional: and to jettison the dynamically existential character of Christian virtue. The fact is that different Christian Churches have interpreted the content and the relevance of the teaching of Jesus differently (in this context), though they have agreed that a sacrificial and personalistic ethic, within marriage, best fulfils itself in a life-long relationship. The rich particularity of human nature, made the more particular by what happens to people in their life-history to date, can create unique situations in response to which some variation from what is usually regarded as normative may well exist. It is *not* always possible to apply the same factual yard-stick to every conceivable human predicament: though the effort to realise a sacrificial love remains, for the Christian, absolute.

How far, and in what personal contexts, the sincere Christian is right to depart from the rule, only that same Christian, under God and seeking the best guidance that he can, is in a position to determine. He must treat himself (and expect others so to treat him) as adult and responsible. He must remember that he belongs to a community and has a responsibility for his brother man. He may often decide, and properly, that in the interests of a *wider* personalism he ought to renounce a more immediate personalism—but this is a decision that only he can make, and others cannot make it for him. A Faith so emphatic in its stress on particularity does not always ask such denial on behalf of universal principles and an overall system. The personal life, capable as it is of such a variety of expression, is so intimate that a few people may find themselves driven beyond and outside (some may say below) the usually accepted standard. What matters basically for such men and women (recognising, of course, how easy is self-deception) is that they should retain their integrity and be honestly seeking the highest realisation of a sacrificial love.

Nor is divorce the only intimate problem which arises out of personal relations between men and women. Birth control, A.I.D. and homosexuality, to mention only three, enter the same personal world. With regard to these, I suspect, no one tidy and overall pattern is either practical or desirable, though the law, in minimal terms, may have to lay one down. The Church standing for a personal order must give guidance. The absolute rejection of birth control, as intrinsically immoral, based on theories as to the "ontological significance of coitus", or the proper fulfilment of a natural function, is I think untenable. There are no precise absolutes in this matter, universally applicable. The extent to which birth control is used, or whether to use it at all, these move in the context of particular situations, social, psychological and so on. To say that "marriage is ordained for the increase of mankind according to the will of God" is to lay down a normative principle: its application needs to be worked out in the light of a man's total (and particular) commitment to glorify God in the relationship of marriage. General advice is helpful: but it is *I* in my unique position, who under God, must apply it.

The same may be true of A.I.D. in respect of which an absolute rejection in *all* circumstances may not be required on purely Christian grounds. It is too early to make a mature judgement, and though it must be admitted that people already need help and guidance (and the state may have to intervene), it is certainly not wise to rush to large pronouncements one way or another. One cannot but remember how the Anglican Church has been forced, in its Lambeth Conferences, to change its mind over birth control. What may be right in a particular, concrete, existential situation may not be equally right for others whose position is far different. What matters again is that they should be trying to realise the intensely personal ethic of Jesus.

To suggest this approach is by no means to advocate an irresponsible subjectivism, nor would it lead to anarchy. It means only that some areas of human life are so intensely personal that except at points where society must take action to ensure the ends for which government exist and to protect those needing protection (and there are of course such situations and such persons), freedom ought to be as wide as possible. "Judge not and ye shall not be judged: condemn not and ye shall not be condemned." Law is concerned primarily with securing a rough justice between man and man, and with the protection of certain social and individual rights. It can easily become tyrannous when it attempts too much, and forgets its limitations. Justice is largely a legal and distributive concept, and therefore in its nature static. Christianity is more concerned with, and indeed much more interested in, dynamic personal relationships. It seeks to lift men out of the area in which law operates and a coercive jurisdiction is necessary into the territory where creative love becomes the controlling loyalty.

No question illustrates more acutely the difficulty sometimes confronting the Christian moralist, and indeed the state legislator for that matter, than that of homosexuality. Modern study has shown that the distinction between male and female is not so absolute as it was once thought to be: and that the obvious physiological distinctions are not the only ones between the sexes. Temperamentally there may well be gradations which move imperceptibly from the one to the other, and society owes a great deal to some of its more feminine men and masculine women. It is therefore difficult to determine precisely what a homosexual relationship is; though the law (where it wishes to intervene) will be forced to make inverted physical relationship the determining factor, particularly since young people must rightly be protected.

Yet it must be frankly admitted that there is a great deal yet to be discovered as to the nature of this continuing phenomenon. How far, for example, is it a permanent condition in some people, and how can this be detected? How and when is it a merely passing phase, indicative of a retarded psychological development?

Here, surely, in respect of particular people, moral judgements must depend on greater factual knowledge on the one hand, and a juster appreciation of individual temperament on the other.

This is not to say that everything ought to be tolerated, for some homosexual relations, as some heterosexual ones, are sinful: and often the "offender" is helped by being treated as a responsible free moral agent who has done "wrong". But it does mean that whatever is properly regarded as normative cannot be applied willy-nilly to all personal contexts; and that hasty condemnation, even if it gives emotional satisfaction to the man who sets himself up as the judge, gives little help to the condemned.

Once again a Christian non-propositional morality, which is always concerned as much with the integrity of the individual as with the "wholeness" of the group, ought to be able to be more sensitive to given situations and less doctrinaire in respect of them than more cut and dried systems. Its over-riding concern is always the fullest possible realisation of a responsible and effective love.

(III)

Some Christians—Hegel and possibly F. D. Maurice—have seen, particularly during the nineteenth century, the state as an absolute. Few today, however, as they look around the world, would see it as such. Indeed the general tendency is to regard the absolute state with suspicion as a dangerous anachronism. The truth seems to be that the nation-state is merely one political order which may well give place to another. Its claims can never be absolute upon the individual or upon the various groupings that live within it.

That some form of political and coercive order is necessary, at least in this phase of man's development, is self-evident: and that it will continue to be so for centuries to come seems equally certain. That any one particular form is an "absolute order", however, the Christian would emphatically question. At a time when a more inclusive order than the nation-state seems to be painfully emerging, the Christian with his committal to history, and his membership in a community which in its nature transcends race and colour, finds no difficulty, or ought to find no difficulty, in moving from one loyalty to another. Any such affirmation as "My country, may she always be in the right: but right or wrong my country" can never be brought within the sanctions of Christian Faith.

The followers of Jesus, at different periods in their history, have found themselves related to society around them in various ways. The clear cut differentiation between Church and State, characteristic of the early days, has been replaced by other and more subtle kinds of inter-relatedness. The fact is that Christianity, through different churches, has incarnated itself in different nations and social patterns in a hundred and one different ways, in response of course to factors of race, temperament, and history.

This inevitably means that the distinction between a man's membership of the Christian Church and his citizenship in the nation is not, in practice, definite and clear cut, and the one often merges into the other. The problem for him, therefore, is not quite so simple as a conflict of loyalties between his

Christian allegiance and his state citizenship. If it were, he would certainly know how to resolve it. Often the two loyalties are inextricably interwoven. Thus J. R. Green writes of the English nation that it was "the child of the Church". It must be confessed that in practice, so strong are the conditioning factors within a modern sovereign state, allegiance to their own nation (a part of their Christian commitment as they see it) has often proved a more critical loyalty than allegiance to a supernational world church.

One of the reasons for this situation is the broken and fragmentary nature of Christendom itself. It is encouraging, in this respect, to notice that there is an increasing awareness by Christians of each other and that schemes for re-union are going forward; though in so far as these efforts are primarily concerned with whether clergymen of church A. may celebrate Holy Communion in Church B. (and vice versa) they seem a little pathetic compared with the gigantic problems facing a universal religious society. Far more serious than the niceties of doctrinal differences is the fact that, at the behest of their respective governments, no common membership of the body of Christ seems able to prevent Christians of different nations, with skill and courage, preparing to blow each other's (and their respective children's) brains out with sustained and ingenious endeavour.

What may be said, with any confidence, in this rather confused field of the nexus between Church and State (in view of the conditioning factors of history) is that there is no one right, or normative, relationship of Christians to the political order, and it is in vain to look for one. To say that the Christian is ultimately bound to obey God rather than man merely lays down a general principle which few will contest simply because it is so general: the difficulty comes when an attempt is made to apply it in particular situations. Here all that can be said is that the individual Christian, using the helps he can, including the guidance that the Church offers him, must finally make up his own mind. There may indeed be systems of government which are so perverse in their ends; which instead of standing for justice, so clearly outrage the most elementary forms of it, that the Christian may feel that he ought (by methods in harmony with, or at least not flagrantly opposed to, his commitment to Jesus) to work for their overthrow. Indeed he may come to believe that a temporary anarchy, with all its possible risks, would be better than the continuation of such a tyranny.

On the other hand, he may be forced realistically to accept that he can do little effectively to change what he condemns; but in this situation he is faced with a serious and indeed unsettling problem. Whatever he does, he cannot deny that he has a responsibility: yet the degree of co-operation which it is proper for a Christian to give to a basically evil political order presents a dilemma which can easily be stated in terms of a slick principle, but is extremely hard to work out in practice. What a Christian feels he must do will depend on his own ability and status, his insights and the nature of the existential situation in which he (and his Church) find themselves. What is rightly expected of the Christian is that, in these resistant contexts, he will still be motivated by an ultimate desire to glorify God in the sacrificial spirit of Jesus.

Wherever he finds himself, he stands under the judgement and the challenge of the Kingdom of God. This is his controlling and regulative loyalty, and his commitment to Jesus must be worked out in the place where he is. A Christian philosophy of the State may over the years help to create a climate of thought and enable him to enter into a continuing corporate knowledge; but it can never decide for him how he must act in his particular position. What may be said in general terms is that, confronted by an evil situation, he will try to make it better: and if he appears to contract out of it, it is still with the same end in view.

In spite of some extreme and eccentric Christian thinking which utterly divorces the state and its morality from the Kingdom and its morality the main stream of the Christian tradition points the other way. What remains doubtful and often ambiguous is the particular way in which the one morality impinges upon or is related to the other. In the modern world where many states—except for strongly Roman Catholic or Communist ones—are neutral in respect of any religious profession, the Christian must work within what he may be tempted to see as a limiting position. Yet the Christian is right to believe that *ultimately* conformity to the divine will (within the context of the collective life) makes for the health of a society. Although he can never regard the state as embodying an "absolute order", he is not content with a "low view" of it, which sees it, in the nature of the case, merely as a coercive instrument, concerned in no way with the good life. If the theocratic ideal, whether it be Hebraic or Platonic, is too lofty and can indeed blur necessary distinctions—which means in practice that efforts to establish it are fraught with the possibility of terrible dangers—yet this need not imply that the state (the nation organised governmentally) is only a necessary nuisance, as some seem to suggest.

Yet the Christian is bound to recognise that there are certain inherent limitations in an order which must use coercive sanctions, and needs to surround its pattern of law with these dread safeguards. The state, as such, cannot by external manipulation, and through positive law, bring to birth the fruits of the spirit, though it may, by treating men as politically responsible, and by allowing groups within the community a measure of creative autonomy, promote the dignity of men. No society, organised governmentally, or church for that matter, is Christian in any full sense, and it is naïve to suggest that it can be. Yet this is not to say that some political orders are not nearer to Christian insights than others. Nazi Germany, in its overall pattern, would seem to be rather a long way away, and the more ruthless expressions of international industrial capitalism not particularly near. For myself, I believe that representative political democracy, no matter how imperfectly realised, does by trying to elicit a free response, and by treating individual people as significant, approach a little nearer to the Kingdom than some other and more monolithic ideologies. "Nearer" but not "within": and democracy itself is subject to its own peculiar abuses and frustrations. The problem inherent in a political order is that if it must see people as potential saints, yet at the same time to be realistic, it has to treat them as actual sinners.

It is of the very essence of the Christian sacrificial way that it must be freely chosen, because a person can never be blitzed or coerced into an effective personal life. This obvious fact must constitute a limitation to the ends which governments can set themselves. There is in all State direction at least a final threat of punitive action, so that it cannot escape a degree, and in some instances a high degree, of impersonality. The Kingdom, in its fullest realisation, knows neither law nor punishment. Thus there remains in the nature of the case a distinction between Church and State, between the deployment of means which may be right for the one but wrong for the other. The danger of the Christian theocratic state, even if one could exist, is that the ethics of the Kingdom cannot be translated into a pattern of positive law. There is no quality of external force which is able to compel people to love one another, even if they are forced to go through the motions of it. The human will is inaccessible to this kind of compulsion. Indeed the mere fact that a State uses a coercive jurisdiction in the supposed interests of religion can weaken an effective witness to the truth that Christianity moves, and must move, in the world of freedom and a joyful filial response.

Yet the Christian recognises the need for an order, for a settled system of government, for the conscious direction of the collective life. He realises the necessity of law, in its right place, and is grateful that the State undertakes much necessary business, not all of it purely utilitarian in character—and he will show his gratitude by entering into responsibility for this necessary discharge of government. The Christian knows only too well from within his own experience that it is helpful to sinful man to live within such restraints as an intelligent law, and an equally intelligent enforcement of it, can impose. Sometimes the Christian will be grateful that the State feels able to declare certain behaviour patterns unlawful, though they do not carry with them any criminal procedure in a court of law. The young man and the weak need protection, physical as well as moral; and sometimes to prevent mob justice law must operate.

But the Christian is all the time conscious of the limitations inherent in collective action, and in the imposition of collective norms—their hit and miss character and so on. He more than any other man is unhappy when law too much invades the primacy of conscience. He recognises that law usually reflects social habits and customs: its concern is to preserve the balance of a status quo; and to prevent the unregenerate passions of men invading individual and collective rights, thereby overturning society.

Archbishop William Temple made much of these limitations in respect of the State. There are many situations, he was prepared to assert, where the most that the State can hope for is to secure justice, and not always a very elevated justice. But the Christian has an interest in justice since not until some elementary pattern of law is established can people living within society pass on to the realisation of love. In a jungle where there is no order, no respect for legal rights, love can hardly be brought to birth at all. The higher rungs of the ethical ladder are only reached by climbing (sometimes clambering) up the lower. A man must first be maintained in his right to justice, before he can sacrifice it in an act of renunciation. A citizen can hardly give away his life, when lawlessness and murder are the "order of the day". To be able to sacrifice oneself means, at one level at least, that one is able to preserve onself.

It must be added, however, that not all Christian moralists would go all the way with the Archbishop in this matter. Indeed some, in certain circumstances, reverse the argument and maintain that there are human situations so anarchical that only such a power as love can beget justice. Nothing else is sufficiently creative or capable of releasing such a maximum of divine power.

(iv)

We are back to the ambiguity with which our discussion in the first chapter began, and to which at present there is no agreed Christian solution. This ambiguity is in part due to the nature of the Christian commitment—existential in and through the concrete situations of everyday life. Such a commitment seeks to realise a Christ-like virtue, self-giving, personalistic and sacrificial. What this means in home and family is not difficult to understand but difficult to live up to. In the cut and thrust of business, and the ordinary economic and political life of society, it is more difficult of application: and in the stubborn field of international relations most difficult of all, though it is essential that it should be applied. A personal ethic is here caught up on the horns of a dilemma: for if its principles are in one sense absolute (e.g. sacrificial personalism—if this may be called a principle) its expression or articulation must be within given contexts. It will be different, for example, in an affluent from a non-affluent society. A welfare state will not only tend to breed a different temper of mind, but will challenge people in new ways.

It is within these different contexts of home, of work, of citizenship that the Christian, by committing himself to them, is led to make his distinctive witness. It is not so much that the insight is relative to the particular situation: but that it is always within the particular situation, and in response to it, that the insight is given.

It is understandable, however, that such reflections should provoke many to ask, almost in exasperation: "When can the Christian as a Christian be definite in respect of particular problems?" Personally, I think there are such occasions and they arise in contexts where particular behaviour patterns flagrantly deny a truth to which Christian Faith is absolutely committed—this truth being fundamental, and the violation of it equally fundamental, in the opposed pattern of behaviour.

"Apartheid" strikes me as a case in point and I quote it merely because it seems capable of just this kind of treatment. Many arguments, of unequal value, have been brought forward on behalf of this particular racial ideology, and its supporters usually claim (and in other contexts the same claim has been put forward in this book) that this social philosophy cannot be meaningfully discussed (or judged) apart from the unique historical situation in response to which it has arisen. Essentially, however, it can hardly be denied that apartheid treats men and women (white as well as black) as members of a class and determines all personal relations between them on a segregated basis. Thus one class in effect says to the other: "We are willing to spend money on you, to educate you, clothe you, feed you etc., but we do not wish to make friends with you, that is, to confront you as persons in effective personal relationships." This absolute refusal, apartheid writes into the law of the land.

As I sit at my desk this moment, I have in front of me a

report in *The Times* newspaper to the effect that a group of coloured and white young South Africans were arrested for having a meal together in a restraurant. Here, it seems to me, is a clear and settled defiance of a precious and vital Christian truth, so much so that even if apartheid were applied in South Africa with more humanity and intelligence than happens to be the case, it would still, in the light of Christian Faith, stand condemned. That men should be free to confront one another at the direct level of a deep encounter; that a man is not merely a representative object but a unique person—this is a basic Christian assertion, not on the periphery of belief but absolutely essential to it. Deny it and Christian Faith becomes so distorted that it ceases almost to be itself. The ethics of Jesus just cannot be made to subserve the pigmentation of a man's skin.

I have quoted the example of apartheid because I believe it to be the least complicated contemporary issue, looked at from the criteria of essential Christian Faith. There are others, where, though I myself think I see an issue clearly, I have to confess that others see it differently, and do not think it possible to isolate one particular factor. An illustration which does not perhaps move in the same world of intense seriousness as the former may be taken from the field of modern advertising which looms ever larger in the contemporary social scene. The whole technique of this system of mass propaganda is geared to the conditioning of people so that they almost necessarily respond in a particular way. The success of the exercise depends on not encouraging a free and responsible choice, and on subtly undermining rational responses. The overall and long-term effects of such a system it is impossible to estimate.

This does not, of course, rule out the possibility that there can be responsible advertising: but it does maintain that certain kinds of techniques are indefensible when seen against the background of a responsible Christian personalism. Once again the anti-personalism is seen as fundamental to certain kinds of advertising. These treat persons at less than a personal level: they deliberately deal with them as things to be used and exploited.

Is it both possible and legitimate to isolate in this way violations of essential Christian insights?—"violation" being understood as such a complete and absolute denial that no process of accommodation or adjustment, or the balancing of one violation against another and choosing the lesser, can hope to compensate. Here, of course, Christian may well disagree with Christian. For myself, I should be prepared to assert that capital punishment is a further example of where this can be done, though Christians have not only sanctioned but often instigated resort to it across the centuries (after the passing of the witness of the early Church). The absolute nature of this punishment represents fallible and sinful man arrogating to himself a sovereignty which belongs only to God. By removing a man deliberately from this terrestrial scene it denies, in practice, the doctrine of divine grace, and does violence to the truth of the Incarnation, which affirms that it is within this time world that God has placed man to work out his salvation "with fear and trembling".

Equally forbidden, so it seems to me—and I am not here raising the question of pacifism from which in my judgement it is separable—is the use and manufacture of hydrogen bombs. I do not believe their deployment can be brought within any system which does not do absolute violence to Christian Faith. For all Christians committed to a personalistic and sacrificial ethic, there must come a point, having made full allowance for necessary adjustments and compromises in this sinful world, beyond which they just cannot go: and they cannot go further because to do so would be to indulge in behaviour patterns which absolutely outrage and indeed contradict the fundamental insights which give substance to the Faith. To indulge in such would constitute a kind of impiety: though God would still work within this impious system to rescue whatever He could from the moral shipwreck, using every sincere man's dedication, caught up in ignorance as this well might be.

Sometimes, I repeat, the Christian must be prepared to find an absolute and to draw a line—though it will not be a propositional absolute, but the absolute of an inner constraint which will not let him go. If there is *no* point beyond which a Christian may not go, then of course no distinctive Christian ethic can be said to exist—indeed hardly any ethic at all. In the hydrogen bomb there is a dimension of violence as is almost absolute in its destructiveness, the end results of which are unpredictable; a weapon so indiscriminately impersonal that I find myself unable to contain it within any Christian commitment whatever.

In adopting this stand, I am painfully conscious, agonisingly conscious, of the weight of "consequential arguments" on the other side, and the inevitable, though as I think rather cheap, charge of irresponsibility. Yet even in a world of relativity, of necessary adjustment, I just cannot go as far as this. I suspect that to cross this Rubicon is to enter the twilight where all the inner-destructiveness of man's unredeemed nature is encouraged to unleash itself in a final Armageddon. To make hydrogen bombs is to be prepared to use them. In such a dilemma, I feel I must fall back on some ultimate conviction as to the nature of Spiritual Reality, and what strikes me as the intuition of Jesus as to how this Final Reality can best be served. I cannot bring myself to believe, even in this sin-infected world, that I must do violence to my deepest moral insights in order to serve my fellow men—let alone God. I dare not assert such a paradox.

I recognise that in respect of the hydrogen bomb the moral judgement made about it in the preceding paragraph derives from an estimate of the consequences of dropping one (widespread destruction and so on); and that this estimate is made without any reference to the intention lying behind the act, i.e. to prevent the consequences which would flow from the domination of the world by communism. Surely, it is said, ought not the two sets of consequences to be factually and morally evaluated, and the lesser of the two evils, in so far as this can be determined, chosen?

This may well be true, but it is important that some distinction be made between these two sets of consequences. The destruction following the dropping of hydrogen bombs is a necessary physical consequence: and no amount of prayer will affect it once such a bomb is in the air heading towards its target. Even the Deity, in the neutral order of nature that He has created and sustains, accepts these consequences and no Christian expects Him to do otherwise. The agents, or the community dropping the bomb, being aware of its certain effects, must be understood as, if not intending them, at least tolerating them.

The consequences flowing from domination by communism are not, however, of the same order. Here there is nothing inevitable and necessary unless we hold that the will of man is in no sense whatever free. Communism, and the results issuing from it, derive from the will of men, perhaps in part from the evil will of men. But men's wills are not inaccessible to other men's wills or to God's over-riding will. Men can and do change from willing evil to willing good. Conversions happen, and it is the Christian conviction that it is part of God's Providence that they should happen. Though the price of bringing this about may prove to be costly in self-sacrifice, the Christian cannot refuse to embark upon it on this account. Indeed it might be claimed that this was his peculiar vocation, and that world domination by communism, tragic though this may be, might present just that challenge of personal confrontation in which Christian Faith and Christian insights come alive, and prove effective. When evil is most virulent, and the challenge most severe, then supremely the Christian falls back on his final beliefs.

Be this as it may, it is important from the Christian point of view not to place on a level the consequences resulting from dropping a hydrogen bomb and the consequences of enslavement from communism. One moves mainly in the world of nature, the other in the world of possible grace. One set of consequences flow necessarily from the act, and cannot be drastically changed by later remedial care. The results from the other, given full allowance for brain washing, etc., remain open, and move in a world accessible to man and God's will. To prefer a closed system of unrestrained violence to an open system of personal confrontation seems, for the Christian, a rather odd choice.

It will be noticed that in what I have said above, I have lapsed, almost unconsciously, into the first person singular. This, I suspect, is significant, and many readers may feel most unfortunate. An act of war, it will be said, is not a personal decision. It is the community that wills it. Is any Christian right in making it a personal decision, and in this respect contracting out of the total life of the society in which he lives?

There of course cannot in the nature of the case ever be any tidy answer to this continuing dilemma, though a great deal which has been said earlier in this book bears upon it. For myself, I believe that there are situations when any mature person is called to make a personal and responsible decision. The collective cannot be absolutely coercive of his will.

To stand over against the community is no light-hearted decision. It ought to be taken only after much thought, discussion, and self-criticism: but when a man finally comes to the point of feeling the compulsion of a deep conviction, there he must finally take his stand. If he does not, it is not himself only who will be impoverished: the community itself will also suffer.

I have quoted two examples (apartheid and advertising) in respect of which, arguing from the premises of Christian Faith, most Christians would probably arrive at the same conclusions. I have quoted two others, giving my own point of view (capital punishment and the hydrogen bomb) where Christian opinion is more evenly divided. Unsatisfactory as this latter situation may be, the Christian can only nourish the hope that so long as such sincere divisions continue, God in His providential ordering of the universe will use every genuine inclination to discover His will, and every committal to it.

Perhaps two more illustrations may be offered (as representative of others) where the vast body of Christian opinion would concur, but where appropriate action would differ according to what the individual Christian felt to be his particular vocation.

Christians, against the background of their sacramental Faith, may well regard the "juice of the grape" as among God's many gifts to men; and as such its right use and enjoyment a means to give God glory. But having said this no Christian can fail to take account of the undoubted fact that no gift is more terribly abused, and consequently causes more widespread misery. What is he to do about this? Some extremists may feel that the attendant evils are so extensive that the trade ought to be suppressed by law—but this would not represent a balanced Christian view. Others may feel that in the interests of their weaker brethren (for whom moderation has ceased to be a safe or possible option), they can best serve them by voluntarily undertaking a total abstinence. Other Christians may equally feel that this is not their way of best witnessing to a right use of God's gifts, and that it is up to them to show that alcohol can be used rightly, responsibly and gratefully.

Here, clearly, are differences of vocation—and both are probably necessary. What the Christian cannot do is to pretend that he has no responsibility for his brother man. The same principles can be applied to gambling. Christians may feel (without deciding the question whether it is in its nature evil) that its social effects are now so injurious upon individuals and the economy generally that they must totally abstain from it. Money represents power over others and to acquire it irresponsibly (in whatever way) is potentially dangerous and corrupting.

The above examples serve to illustrate the different situations in which Christians live, and the different responses which they (and sometimes the same Christians) make to them. What must be clear is that what is fitting for the Christian himself to undertake in the light of his Faith—the Christian who is prepared to die to live—may not be equally fitting, or possible, for a community which is not committed to a particular Christian ethic. The case of total abstinence as a vocation for some Christians underlines this point. Even if a Christian witness were unanimous here, it would not be right for the State to insist upon such a denial (as it rightly does in the drug trade) unless the resulting evils (which stand over against the obvious pleasures) were much greater. The Christian ethic of renunciation, the essence of which is that it is voluntary, *cannot be written into law.*

This means that for the Christian, and indeed for the Christian community, there must be a measure of adjustment to the world in which a common humanity lives. This is the truth implicit in the realistic ethical view to which we have called attention earlier. In some situations the personal content of a possible Christian witness is inevitably lowered, and this is more usually the case where the collective life is concerned, and particularly in its coercive responsibilities.

Yet the real tragedy, and this is painfully evident, is that the process of adjustment has gone too far, scandalously beyond what was necessary and that the Christian has tended to forget that when evil is most virulent, he ought the more particularly to feel the challenge of his Faith, and to fall back upon it. Failure to do this has meant, in practice, that he has often found it difficult to take up his stand anywhere. The cutting edge of a Christian witness has thereby been blunted.

The Inquisition and the Slave Trade are cases in point. Though it may seem charitable to assert that these abuses must be assessed against the background of the age: yet the age itself was in part generated by the Christian Church; and that same Church earlier in its history absolutely condemned torture, and would not tolerate violence of any kind. It is indeed an extraordinary phenomenon that a Church holding such definite views at one time should itself have taken the lead in encouraging barbarity at another. For myself I am convinced that a more positive stand, from within the thought forms of the Faith (ambiguously escapist as it might appear), would in the long run have proved more practically effective. It is a fact of history that Christ's unambiguous moral witness has done more than anything else to change the pattern of men's lives.

Postscript

The varying problems inherent in relating the personalistic ethic of Jesus to contemporary living have been commented upon in this chapter more to illustrate the nature of the exercise than to provide cut and dried answers to immediate questions. Sometimes it has not been easy to see precisely how a sacrificial ethic can be brought to bear upon particular situations, that is how the example of Jesus may be made directly relevant. It is for this reason that throughout the discussion there remains the perennial question: What is the relationship of the ethics of the Kingdom of God, as Jesus proclaimed them, to everyday life?

To lighten this difficulty, some theologians have suggested that the example and ethical precepts of Jesus constituted only an "interim ethic". According to such a view, Jesus, the unique

Messianic Servant, came to usher in the Kingdom of God, and his ethic, therefore, is that of God's reign when in its perfection it is eschatalogically realised. We, his followers, who live in the world, and on *this* side of the Kingdom, cannot hope to realise this perfection. For us, the "end" is not yet. Thus Dr. Wilhelm Hermann ("Essays on the Social Gospel") goes so far as to maintain: "Efforts to imitate Jesus in points inseparable from his historic mission in the world and of his position—which is not ours—efforts like these, lacking the sincerity of really necessary tasks, have so long injured the cause of Jesus that our joy will be unalloyed when scientific study at last reveals to everyone the impossibility of all such attempts."

Dr. Martin Dibelius, though not going quite so far, writes: "The typical example of the New Testament message is the Sermon on the Mount. The words of Jesus of which it consists were originally spoken to announce God's absolute will without reference to the circumstances of the world, their conditions and their requirement. Thus these words give expression to the law of the coming Kingdom of God."

In a short work of this kind, it is impossible to give the theological pros and cons for this point of view. Suffice to say that its acceptance depends on a particular interpretation of so much that is in debate in the field of eschatology that its conclusions must remain, to say the least, precarious. Also it must be remembered that the authors of the Gospel obviously regarded the ethical teaching and moral example of Jesus as sufficiently significant to devote a great deal of space to them. Perhaps it is not too much to say that unless the first disciples had found a supreme "virtue" in Jesus, they would never have been moved to accept him as the unique servant of God. It was his transcendental goodness which made it possible for them to see him as fulfilling a long expected historic mission.

Others who have thought long and deeply over this same

problem reluctantly persuade themselves that the ethic of Jesus is directly relevant only to those areas of human life which are intimate and personal. The attempt to introduce this ethic into the more resistant and far less flexible territory of the collective life—to nations and society as a whole where the grim fact of coercive power necessarily looms larger—can be almost disastrous. An extreme expression of this point of view is given by Dr. Charles Mercier, who divides the sphere of ethics into the "moral" and the "patriotic", and maintains that the commands of Jesus are applicable only to the former—that is to the private relations of citizens to one another.

From such a mood, a Christian indifference to Nazism may all too easily spring.

Dr. Reinhold Niebuhr writes in more restrained language: "Love is not an immediate possibility in the larger and more indirect relations of life. It is an illusion of liberal Protestantism that the Ethics of the Sermon on the Mount can be made immediately applicable to these relationships."

A less academic, and what its exponents would regard as a more common-sense point of view, maintains that the more challenging and "hard" sayings of Jesus must be interpreted metaphorically, and obeyed in the "spirit" rather than in the "letter"—a thesis which seems rather self-evident, since the teaching of Jesus obviously cannot be applied by rule of thumb to contemporary situations. Yet in so far as this approach tends to take the power out of his teaching, it is to be deplored. One is reminded of Gore's comment that such a view too easily encourages a man to observe neither the letter nor the spirit.

So are we forced to conclude that ambiguity is rooted in a Faith which bids men conquer the "world": to handle power: to build a Kingdom—and yet at the same time challenges them to do this with a cross and under the leadership of a sacrificial Christ who died upon it. Sometimes—and it is useless to deny this—such ambiguity makes a distinctive witness difficult and gives rise to a variety of personal commitments. At least there is some comfort in the thought that the difficulty results from the conviction that the Christian is concerned with the world and must be dynamically active about it. If he were to turn his back on the "orders" this particular problem would disappear: but Christians rightly seek to contribute to the direction of society around them. Christian historicism makes psychological escapism impossible: as can be seen in a robust common sense which is slowly but surely rejecting the blasphemous and wholly perverse contention that "it would be better to be wiped out than to live under Communism". This is not martyrdom but nihilism: it does not seek to direct history but to abolish it: it does not consummate but destroys.

It is, then, within this world that the Christian is called upon to make his Christian decisions—such decisions arising from his total commitment. Through his worship, his meditation upon the Scriptures and his life of prayer, he becomes aware of, sometimes is constrained by, the intimations of a will greater than his own. Such a confrontation drives him to repentance and in this experience he sees how partial and at times how fitful are both his awareness and his response. Yet he offers himself to this will; and within the situations where he is, and seeking all the guidance he can from a continuing Christian experience and the discipline of facts, he decides and he takes action.

As a Christian, he knows that he lives always under the judgement of God's perfect Kingdom: and he can never forget this, even in his moments of greatest achievement. Always the Kingdom, with Jesus as its Lord, remains to rebuke pride, to challenge, to support and to inspire.

But this gap, this "great divide" must not be accepted with complacency as in the nature of things, but only as in the nature of a sinful humanity. If indeed Christianity is to direct the course of the future, thereby bringing the world nearer to the Kingdom of God, Christians will *have* to realise a higher virtue, and to incarnate it in a rapidly changing world.

A technological age means, inevitably, increasing centralisation, increasing conditioning of man by the techniques of modern industrialism—and this must continue if the world is to be fed and humanity as a whole lifted out of the blight of poverty and the misery of ignorance. Yet such a pattern *does* present challenges, particularly to an ideology which is basically and intensely personal. The long-term effects of such technology upon the psychology of man we do not as yet know; though the inability of the churches of Christendom at present to win the industrial worker is only too painfully evident. One thing that Marxism has taught us (or reminded us of) is the solidarity of the class structure engendered by men working together in industry at a common level. What this "thing" Christianity means in such a context, what its ethical demand is, it would not be easy to say. "Production for use and not for profit" is a stirring war cry but how far the antithesis is a real one is open to question. If the machine seems to depersonalise, yet it might be held that the man in charge of the machine develops a certain "know-how", with a resulting self-respect. When released from his work he is the more anxious to fulfil himself in his personal life (for which he has greater leisure). Certainly a faith (in spite of the fact that some of the mediaevals saw work as a result of the "Fall") cannot, in the light of its incarnational teaching and the example of a Christ who was thankful that he had finished the work that God had given him to do, fail to see a man's labour as significant—a means in and through which he may glorify God and enter into worth-while relations with, and contribute to the welfare of, his fellow men.

One thing is certain. Christians are not to look back nostalgically over their shoulders to lament a lost Eden. They must see the new age, with all its perils and denials, as in part resulting from those dynamic energies which their own Faith has encouraged. If there are difficulties, there are also wonderful opportunities. Here is a new territory to invade and ethically to subdue: and to swing into the orbit of the Kingdom.

If this is to happen, however, that is if Christianity is to witness to a more final order, Christians will have to sharpen their impact and assert the ethical uniqueness of their Faith. To allow a too accommodating spirit progressively to dull its cutting edge is a grand betrayal. A steady endeavour to enlarge the area in which a sacrificial personalism can be made effective is the supreme task confronting the Church in these days. It must at all costs reassert a specialised vocation. The communists have worked out a social ethic expressive of their beliefs. Christians must do the same. The time in which to do this may be shorter than we think.

Wed, 13ᵗʰ December.